50 Science Zingers!

Written & Illustrated by B. K. Hixson

Published by Loose in the Lab, Inc.
9462 South 560 West
Sandy, Utah 84070

www.looseinthelab.com

*Library of Congress
Cataloging-in-Publication Data
Available Upon Request*

Printed in the United States of America
Ooh aah be bop a lulah!

Dedication

The Yar Yar Logars • '78–'80
(Weatherford Hall • 3/4 East • OSU)

Here's to Jimmy Buffet, ultimate Frisbee, rippin' up the Mary's Peak Marathon relay, cocktail hour at the end of the hall, graffiti in the freight elevator, sorority dances, basketball games at Gill, lunar eclipses on the balcony, spring football in the mud, tubbing contests, steak night, dances on the cafeteria roof—and all of the other diversions that accompanied our higher education.

Gentlemen, it was a pleasure to live with you and share those most memorable of years—college. Many happy memories to come and many years to enjoy those that we have accumulated.

Acknowledgments

Getting a book out for public consumption is far from a one-man job. There are lots of thank-yous to be doodled out and at the risk of leaving someone out, we attempt to do that on this page. In terms of my chemistry education I was first exposed to ideas in grade school by Mr. Goffard, my fifth grade teacher, and my dad loved to quiz me about the periodic table of the elements. I think we may have mixed something up in junior high school. My real education started when I discovered a chemistry cabinet in the teaching lab at Oregon State University. It looked like it hadn't been used for a couple of decades and that seemed to be the concensus amoung the faculty who also granted me unrestricted permission to play with the contents. Needless to say that is when my real chemistry education began as I accidentally started my hand on fire with red phosphorous, created contact explosives, experimented with permanent dyes and indicators that changed all kinds of colors. What an adventure!

As for my educational outlook, the hands-on perspective, and the use of humor in the classroom, Dr. Fox, my senior professor at Oregon State University, gets the credit for shaping my educational philosophy while simultaneously recognizing that even at the collegiate level we were on to something a little different. He did his very best to encourage, nurture, and support me while I was getting basket loads of opposition for being willing to swim upstream. There were also several colleagues who helped to channel my enthusiasm during those early, formative years of teaching: Dick Bishop, Dick Hinton, Dee Strange, Connie Ridgway, and Linda Zimmermann. Thanks for your patience, friendship, and support.

Next up are all the folks that get to do the dirty work that make the final publication look so polished but very rarely get the credit they deserve. Our resident graphics guru Kris Barton gets a nod for scanning and cleaning the artwork you find on these pages, as well as putting together the graphics that make up the cover. A warm Yankee yahoo to Sue Moore our editor who passes her comments on so that Kathleen Hixson and Sue Moore (once again) can take turns simultaneously proofreading the text while mocking my writing skills.

Once we have a finished product, it has to be printed so that Jay Brochu, Louisa Walker, Tracy St. Pierre, and the Delta Education gang can market and ship the books, and collect the money.

Mom and Dad, as always, get the end credits. Thanks for the education, encouragement, and love. And for Kathy and the kids—Porter, Shelby, Courtney, and Aubrey—hugs and kisses.

50 Science Zingers! • B. K. Hixson

Repro Rights

There is very little about this book that is truly formal, but at the insistence of our wise and esteemed counsel, let us declare: *No part of this book may be reproduced or utilized in any form or by any means, electronic or mechanical, including photocopying, recording, or by any information storage and retrieval system, without permission in writing from the publisher.* That would be us.

More Legal Stuff

Official disclaimer for you aspiring scientists and lab groupies. This is a hands-on science book. By the very intent of the design, you will be directed to use common, nontoxic, household items in a safe and responsible manner to avoid injury to yourself and others who are present while you are pursuing your quest for knowledge and enlightenment in the world of chemistry. Just make sure that you have a fire blanket handy and a wall-mounted video camera to corroborate your story.

If, for some reason, perhaps even beyond your own control, you have an affinity for disaster, we wish you well. *But we, in no way take any responsibility for any injury that is incurred to any person using the information provided in this book or for any damage to personal property or effects that are directly or indirectly a result of the suggested activities contained herein.* Translation: You're on your own, despite the fact that many have preceded you in the lab. Take heed from our friend Johnny, who was a chemist, but is a chemist no more. For what he thought was H_2O was H_2SO_4.

Less Formal Legal Stuff

If you happen to be a home schooler or very enthusiastic school teacher please feel free to make copies of this book for your classroom or personal family use—one copy per student, up to 35 students. If you would like to use an experiment from this book for a presentation to your faculty or school district, we would be happy to oblige. Just give us a whistle and we will send you a release for the particular lab activity you wish to use. Please contact us at the address below. Thanks.

Special Requests
Loose in the Lab, Inc.
9462 South 560 West
Sandy, Utah 84070

Table of Contents

The National Content Standards (K–4)

• *Scientific investigations involve asking and answering a question and comparing the answer with what scientists already know about the world.*

• *Scientists use different kinds of investigations depending on the questions that you are trying to answer. Types of investigation include describing objects, events, and organisms; classifying them; and doing a fair test (experimenting).*

• *Scientists develop explanations using observations (evidence) and what they already know about the world (scientific knowledge). Good explanations are based on evidence from investigations.*

• *Scientists review and ask questions about the results of other scientists' work.*

My All-Time Favorite Zinger

My Top 10 Zingers

The Best of the Rest

Water Zingers

Air Zingers

Heat Zingers

Table of Contents

Classical Mechanics Zingers

Who Are You? And ...

First of all, we may have an emergency at hand and we'll both want to cut to the chase and get the patient into the cardiac unit if necessary. So, before we go too much further, **define yourself**. Please check one and only one choice listed below and then immediately follow the directions that follow *in italics*. Thank you in advance for your cooperation.

I am holding this book because ...

   A. I am a responsible, but panicked, parent. My son / daughter / triplets (circle one) just informed me that his / her / their science fair project is due tomorrow. This is the only therapy I could afford on such short notice. Which means that if I were not holding this book, my hands would be encircling the soon-to-be-worm-bait's neck.

Directions: Can't say this is the first or the last time we heard that one. Hang in there, we can do this.

1. Quickly read the Table of Contents with the worm bait. The headers describe what each section is about. Obviously, the kid is not passionate about science or you would not be in this situation. See if you can find an idea that causes some portion of an eyelid or facial muscle to twitch.

If that does not work, we recommend narrowing the list to the following labs because they are fast, use materials that can be acquired with limited notice, and the intrinsic level of interest is generally quite high.

50 Science Zingers! • B. K. Hixson

How to Use This Book

2. *Take the materials list from the lab write-up and page 207 of the Surviving a Science Fair Project section and go shopping.*

3. *Assemble the materials and perform the lab at least once. Gather as much data as you can.*

4. *Go to page 184 and start on Step 1 of Preparing Your Science Fair Project. With any luck you can dodge an academic disaster.*

___ **B. I am worm bait.** My science fair project is due tomorrow and there is not anything moldy in the fridge. I need a big Band-Aid, in a hurry.

Directions: Same as Option A. You can decide if and when you want to clue your folks in on your current dilemma.

___ **C. I am the parent of a student who informed me that he/ she has been assigned a science fair project due in six to eight weeks.** My son/daughter has expressed an interest in science books with humorous illustrations that attempt to explain physical science and associated phenomena.

Who Are You? And ...

Directions: Well, you came to the right place. Give your kids these directions and stand back.

A. The first step is to read through the Table of Contents and see if anything grabs your interest. Read through several experiments, see if the science teacher has any of the more difficult materials to acquire like aluminum rods, convection carafes, and some of the chemicals, and ask if they can be borrowed. Play with the experiments and see which one really tickles your fancy.

B. After you have found and conducted the experiment that you like, take a peek at the Science Fair Ideas and see if you would like to investigate one of those or create an idea of your own. The guidelines for those are listed on page 193 in the Surviving Your Science Fair section. You have plenty of time so you can fiddle and fool with the original experiment and its derivations several times. Work until you have an original question you want to answer, and then start the process listed on page 198. You are well on your way to an excellent grade.

___D. I am a responsible student and have been assigned a science fair project due in six to eight weeks. I am interested in physics and, despite demonstrating maturity and wisdom well beyond the scope of my peers, I too still have a sense of humor. Enlighten and entertain me.

Directions: Cool. Being teachers, we have heard reports of this kind of thing happening but usually in an obscure and hard-to-locate town several states removed. Nonetheless, congratulations.

Same as Option C. You have plenty of time and should be able to score very well. We'll

How to Use This Book

keep our eyes peeled when the Nobel Prizes are announced in a couple of years.

___ **E. I am a parent who home schools my child/children.** We are always on the lookout for quality curriculum materials that are not only educationally sound but kid- and teacher-friendly. I am not particularly strong in science but I realize it is a very important topic. How is this book going to help me out?

Directions: In a lot of ways we created this book specifically for home schoolers.

1. We break down the experiments in the book and tell you the major ideas that you would want your kid to know. Some people call them objectives, others call them curriculum standards, educational benchmarks, or assessment norms. Same apple, different name. The bottom line is that when your children are done studying this unit on physics you want them to not only understand and explain each of the labs listed in this book, but also be able to defend and argue their position based on experiential evidence, hands-on science, that they have collected.

2. We have collected and rewritten 50 hands-on science labs. Each one has been specifically selected so that it supports significant ideas. This is critical. As the kids do the science experiment, they see, smell, touch, and hear it. They will store that information in several places in their brains. When it comes time to comprehend the idea of the lab, the concrete hands-on experiences provide the foundation for building the idea, which is quite often abstract. Kids who merely read about electromagnetism, fluid dynamics, and momentum, notice the transfer of static charge, or overhear someone describing the rapid oxidation of potassium permanganate, are trying to build abstract ideas on abstract ideas and quite often miss the mark.

Who Are You? And ...

*For example: I can show you a recipe in a book for chocolate chip cookies and ask you to reiterate it. Or I can turn you loose in a kitchen, have you mix the ingredients, grease the pan, plop the dough on the cookie sheet, slide everything into the oven and wait impatiently until they pop out eight minutes later. Chances are that the description given by the person who actually made the cookies is going to be much better based on their true understanding of the process, **founded in experience.***

4. Once you have completed the experiment, there are a number of extension ideas under Take It and Run with It that allow you to spend as much or as little time on the ideas as you deem necessary.

5. A word about humor. Science is not usually known for being funny even though Bill Nye The Science Guy, *Beaker from* Sesame Street, *and* Beakman's World *do their best to mingle the two. That's all fine and dandy but we want you to know that we incorporate humor because it is scientifically (and educationally) sound to do so. Plus it's really at the root of our personalities. Here's what we know:*

When we laugh ...
a. Our pupils dilate, increasing the amount of light entering the eye.
b. Our heart rate increases, which pumps more blood to the brain.
c. Oxygen rich blood to the brain means the brain is able to collect, process, and store more information. Big I.E.: increased comprehension.
d. Laughter relaxes muscles, which can be involuntarily tense if a student is uncomfortable or fearful of an academic topic.
e. Laughter stimulates the immune system, which will ultimately translate into overall health and fewer kids who say they are sick of science.
f. Socially, it provides an acceptable pause in the academic routine, which then gives students time to regroup and prepare to address some of the more difficult ideas with a renewed spirit. They can study longer and focus on ideas more efficiently.
g. Laughter releases chemicals in the brain that are associated with pleasure and joy.

6. If you follow each section of the book in the order it is written, you will be able to build ideas and concepts in a logical and sequential pattern. But that is by no means necessary. For a complete set of guidelines on our ideas on how to teach home schooled kids science, check out our book, Why's the Cat on Fire? How to Excel at Teaching Science to Your Home Schooled Kids.

How to Use This Book

___ F. **I am a public/private school teacher** and this looks like an interesting book to add ideas to my classroom lesson plans.

Directions: It is, and please feel free to do so. However, while this is a great classroom resource for kids, may we also recommend one other title that can be found in a teacher oriented resource book titled Science Never Sucks *(Grades K–6).*

This book has teacher preparation pages, student response sheets or lab pages, lesson plans, bulletin board ideas, discovery center ideas, vocabulary sheets, unit pretests, unit exams, lab practical exams, and student grading sheets. Basically everything you need if you are a science nincompoop, and a couple of cool ideas if you are a seasoned veteran with an established curriculum. All of the ideas that are covered in this one book are covered much more thoroughly in the other. It was specifically written for teachers.

___ G. **My son/daughter/grandson/niece/father-in-law** is interested in science, and this looks like fun.

Directions: Congratulations on your selection. Add a gift certificate to the local science supply store and a package of hot chocolate mix and you have the perfect rainy Saturday afternoon gig.

___ H. **Being members of the SFSPJ (Society for Spontaneous Practical Jokes) we were wondering if you could send us your favorite recipe for contact explosives? We were thinking of a toilet seat stopper application.**

Directions: Nope. Try the Anarchist's Cookbook *and be sure to put it on wet, rather than dry.*

Lab Safety

Contained herein are 50 science activities to help you better understand the nature and characteristics of physics as we currently understand these things. However, since you are on your own in this journey we thought it prudent to share some basic wisdom and experience in the safety department.

Read the Instructions

An interesting concept, especially if you are a teenager. Take a minute before you jump in and get going to read all of the instructions as well as the warnings. If you do not understand something, stop and ask an adult for help.

Clean Up All Messes

Keep your lab area clean. It will make it easier to put everything away at the end and may also prevent contamination and the subsequent germination of a species of mutant tomato bug larva. You will also find that chemicals perform with more predictability if they are not poisoned with foreign molecules.

Organize

Translation: Put it back where you get it. If you need any more clarification, there is an opening at the landfill for you.

HELLO.

GOODBYE.

Dispose of Poisons Properly

This will not be much of a problem with the labs that are suggested in this book. However, if you happen to wander over into one of the many disciplines that incorporates the use of more advanced chemicals, then we would suggest that you use great caution with the materials and definitely dispose of any and all poisons properly.

Practice Good Fire Safety

If there is a fire in the room, notify an adult immediately. If an adult is not in the room and the fire is manageable, smother the outbreak with a fire blanket or use a fire extinguisher. When the fire is contained, immediately send someone to find an adult. If, for any reason, you happen to catch on fire, **REMEMBER: Stop, Drop, and Roll.** Never run; it adds oxygen to the fire, making it burn faster, and it also scares the bat guano out of the neighbors when they see the neighbor kids running down the block doing an imitation of a campfire marshmallow without the stick.

Protect Your Skin

It is a good idea to always wear protective gloves whenever you are working with chemicals. Again, this particular book does not suggest or incorporate hazardous chemicals in its lab activities. This is because we are primarily incorporating only safe, manageable kinds of chemicals for these labs. If you do happen to spill a chemical on your skin, notify an adult immediately and then flush the area with water for 15 minutes. It's unlikely, but if irritation develops, have your parents or another responsible adult look at it. If it appears to be of concern, contact a physician. Take any information that you have about the chemical with you.

Lab Safety

Save Your Nose Hairs

Sounds like a cause celebre L.A. style, but it is really good advice. To smell a chemical to identify it, hold the open container six to ten inches down and away from your nose. Make a clockwise circular motion with your hand over the opening of the container, "wafting" some of the fumes toward your nose. This will allow you to safely smell some of the fumes without exposing yourself to a large dose of anything noxious. This technique may help prevent a nosebleed or your lungs from accidentally getting burned by chemicals.

Wear Goggles If Appropriate

If the lab asks you to heat or mix chemicals, be sure to wear protective eyewear. Also have an eyewash station or running water available. You never know when something is going to splatter, splash, or react unexpectedly. It is better to look like a nerd and be prepared than schedule a trip down to pick out a Seeing Eye dog. If you do happen to accidentally get chemicals in your eye, flush the area for 15 minutes. If any irritation or pain develops, immediately go see a doctor.

Lose the Comedy Routine

You should have plenty of time scheduled during your day to mess around, but science lab is not one of them. Horseplay breaks glassware, spills chemicals, and creates unnecessary messes—things that parents do not appreciate. Trust us on this one.

No Eating

Do not eat while performing a lab. Putting your food in the lab area contaminates your food and the experiment. This makes for bad science and worse indigestion. Avoid poisoning yourself and goobering up your lab ware by observing this rule.

Happy and safe experimenting!

Recommended Materials Suppliers

For every lesson in this book we offer a list of materials. Many of these are very easy to acquire, and if you do not have them in your home already, you will be able to find them at the local grocery or hardware store. For more difficult items we have selected, for your convenience, a small but respectable list of suppliers who will meet your needs in a timely and economical manner. Call for a catalog or quote on the item that you are looking for, and they will be happy to give you a hand.

Loose in the Lab
9462 South 560 West
Sandy, Utah 84070
Phone 1-888-403-1189
Fax 1-801-568-9586
www.looseinthelab.com

Delta Education
80 NW Boulevard
Nashua, NH 03601
Phone 1-800-442-5444
Fax 1-800-282-9560
www.delta-education.com

Nasco
901 Jonesville Ave.
Fort Atkinson, Wisconsin 53538
Phone 1-414-563-2446
Fax 1-920-563-8296
www.nascofa.com

Ward's Scientific
5100 W Henrietta Road
Rochester, New York 14692
Phone 1-800-387-7822
Fax 1-716-334-6174
www.wardsci.com

Educational Innovations
151 River Road
Cos Cob, CT 06807
Phone 1-888-912-7474
Fax 1-203-629-2739
www.teachersource.com

Frey Scientific
100 Paragon Parkway
Mansfield, OH 44903
Phone 1-800-225-FREY
Fax 1-419-589-1546
www.freyscientific.com

Fisher Scientific
485 S. Frontage Rd.
Burr Ridge, Il 60521
Phone 1-800-955-1177
Fax 1-800-955-0740
www.fisheredu.com

Flinn Scientific
PO Box 219
Batavia, Il 60510
Phone 1-800 452-1261
Fax 1-630-879-6962
www.flinnsci.com

The Ideas,
Lab Activities,
& Science Fair
Extensions

What Is a Zinger?

When you present a short, "ooh aah" experiment that makes your friends sit upright in their chairs, provokes thought, and then reaches out and twists handfuls of exposed neurons until they scream, you have just uncorked a zinger. Zingers are fun. They stink, they float, they ooze—they almost certainly evoke smiles and laughter if done right. They stem from the philosophy that we believe that good science education should occasionally take on the guise of performance art.

So, by now, you are a little curious about the origin of the term "zingers." My first year of prolonged coronary thrombosis took place in a junior high science room in Tigard, Oregon. It was there that I was paid a meager sum of money to voluntarily subject myself to the tormenting of 150 hormonally distraught seventh graders—and, frankly, it was a less than stellar start to a teaching career. But one Friday—and I have yet to talk with the Vatican, but I am sure this qualified under one of the "Minor Miracle" clauses, my sixth period class, all of whom I was certain would serve some time in a correctional facility, completed a lab activity flawlessly. To reward this supreme effort on their part, I told them that I'd do a… a… zinger (for lack of imagination I looked down and noticed the wrapper that had previously contained the dessert of the same name that I had recently ingested).

Initially, they were somewhat skeptical about this supposed "reward," but when I told them I would show them how to create a fire by mixing two chemicals and they realized that they were finally going to learn a valuable life skill during school time, they sat right up and paid attention. I pulled the goodies out that I needed and created spontaneous combustion. They loved the science. To my stunned disbelief, they cheered and applauded wildly—and right then and there I had discovered my own personal sanity guarantee.

You are holding, in your hands, a collection of 50 of my favorite experiments. They are all fun, they will be very entertaining for your friends, they all teach science, and every one of them can be turned into a spectacular science fair project. Have fun.

Cornstarch Fireballs

A Little Background

This was the very first zinger that I used in the classroom and remains my all-time favorite for several reasons. One, it produces a huge, relatively harmless, ball of fire that everyone loves to see. Two, everyone absolutely loves it and is immediately hooked on zingers. And, three, it is an excellent way to introduce fire safety, lab safety, and classroom expectations if you are a home schooler, teacher, or science enthusiast with a little too much time on your hands.

This zinger also epitomizes the essence of what a zinger is. It is short, generates a very high level of interest, and uses common, easy-to-find materials. In sort, cornstarch is blown through a paper tube into the flame of a propane torch or Bunsen burner and ignites, producing a fireball that is several feet long and guaranteed to impress everyone in the room.

Setting the Trap ...

Invite a friend to help with your demonstration and ask him to place a pair of goggles over his eyes and a pair of heavy gloves over his hands (leather gardening gloves work fine). Once he is outfitted, ask him to hold his hands together in front of him, palms up, and place a sheet of paper on his palms. Open a box of cornstarch and pour a pile in the middle of the paper, turn to your volunteer and ask him if he has ever been blown up. The answer is usually "No," and I reply, "Good, this will be your first time then." Most all of your audience will laugh, but *everyone* in the room is watching everything you do because they think you are going to blow this kid up.

Props

2   Pair of goggles
1   Pair of gloves, heavy
1   Propane torch w/ignitor
1   Sheet of paper
1   Box of cornstarch
1   Fire blanket or fire extinguisher
    Adult Supervision

The Zing!

1. Goggles on both of you, and gloves on your assistant—sets a good example. Light the propane torch and set it next to the kid who will be your assistant. The flame needs to be as big as you can make it.

2. Pick the torch up and lean over your assistant who is holding the paper with the cornstarch. Attempt to light it on fire with the torch. It will brown but not catch on fire because there is not enough oxygen present to reach the kindling point. Look puzzled.

3. Take the paper from the kid and hand then him the torch.

4. Roll the paper up with the cornstarch on the inside. Ask the kid to hold the torch up and away from his head. I tell him to look like the Statue of Liberty.

5. Darken the room, stand about 3 feet from the flame, take a breath, and blow the cornstarch out of the tube and just above the flame. It will ignite and a large flame will delight your audience. There is a cartoon on the top of the next page that shows you how to set this up so that it is safe and successful.

Cornstarch Fireballs

Things I've Screwed Up

1. <u>Very Important!</u> Breathe in *before* you put the tube of cornstarch to your lips. This may seem like an idiotic piece of advice to you, but the second or third time I demonstrated this idea to a pile of kids I did just that. I placed the tube in my mouth and then took a deep breath. Bad idea. My eyes bugged out. I belched out a huge gasp of air, cornstarch went all over the classroom, and the kids were falling out of their chairs laughing while my eyes watered over to the point where I could not see and I was having severe pulmonary dysfunction.

2. Emphasize that the kid holding the torch can scream, piddle in his shorts, or even close his eyes, but he must hang on to the torch. I have never had a kid drop a torch, but I did have one throw it to me after the experiment was over.

3. Aim about a foot above the flame. If you send the bulk of the cornstarch right at the nozzle tip, you will probably extinguish the flame and get modest combustion of the cornstarch. Aiming higher allows the cornstarch to disperse, creating a larger surface area and a flame about 4 to 6 feet long. Guaranteed "ooh aah."

How Come, Huh?

In order for there to be a sustained fire you have to have three things: heat (provided by the torch), fuel (the cornstarch), and oxygen to assist with the combustion.

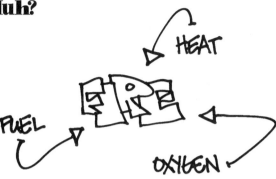

When you tried to ignite the pile of cornstarch, it did not work because there was not enough air available to ignite the cornstarch—it was packed too tight.

The cornstarch burst into flames when it was blown through the tube because blowing the cornstarch into the air mixed it with the oxygen, and there was a lot more surface area of the fuel exposed as well. The more surface area that is exposed, the more opportunity there is for a chemical reaction between the cornstarch and the oxygen, which in this case is combustion. If there is not enough oxygen, there won't be any fire.

Take It & Run with It

1. Another fun way to make a huge fireball quickly is to use lycopodium powder. It is the dried spore of a certain species of club moss. Have your volunteer hold the torch away from herself. Take a handful and throw it down and away from both of you. It will produce a huge flame. See *Le Boom du Jour* for complete instructions.

My Top 10 Favorite Zingers

The Surprise Fire

A Little Background

This lab is in a virtual dead heat with Cornstarch Fireballs on page 22 as my all-time favorite. The only thing really separating the two is that Cornstarch Fireballs was the very first experiment that I did for kids when I started teaching and it is always a favorite.

This is the experiment that I referenced on page 21 where we discuss just what a zinger is and how it can save your bacon. I did this for my 6th period class to save my sanity and have done it hundreds of times since for classes, assemblies, workshops, and all of my nieces and nephews at every family camping trip. It's a winner, your friends will love it, especially if you are putting on a science show. Oxidation comes alive in a heartbeat for everyone.

Props

1   1 oz. Bottle of glycerin
1   1 oz. Bottle of potassium permanganate
2   Pairs of goggles
1   Tart pan
1   Napkin
     Water
     Adult Supervision

The Zing!

1. Place a wet paper towel under an *inverted* tart pan in a **well-ventilated** area. Make a small volcano in the center of the tart pan using potassium permanganate. The volcano should be no more than 2 inches in diameter.

The Surprise Fire

2. Have the kid who made the volcano show his hand to the audience. There is no effect when skin comes in contact with this chemical for a brief period of time.

3. Have another assistant taste a small taste of glycerin. Make a hole in the center of the volcano with your thumb and carefully fill the hole of the volcano with glycerin until it starts to flow down the side of the volcano. Wait 15 to 30 seconds and the show will begin.

4. There will be a poof of smoke followed immediately by a large yellow-blue flame. It will burn for about 20 to 30 seconds and the kids will "ooh" and "aah" the whole time.

Do not touch the tart pan, it gets very hot—and, once again, make sure that you are in a well-ventilated area.

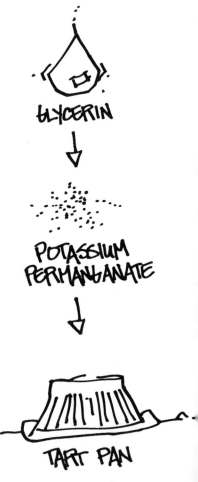

GLYCERIN

POTASSIUM PERMANGANATE

TART PAN

5. When the fire has died out, ask the kid who held the potassium permanganate to show his hand to everyone. No holes? Ask the kid who tasted the glycerin to stick her tongue out. No mutation? Explain that it is very important to clean up messes, especially chemical ones, because you never know when they are going to react with one another. In this case if they are separate, no problem, but if he were to put his hand in her mouth (pointing to your assistants)... pause for effect... and your friends will all start to laugh.

Things I've Screwed Up

Temperature is very important in chemical reactions. I was preparing to do an assembly one winter morning in Utah and as is typical it was in the low teens. I had left all of my materials, including the chemicals in the truck overnight. I set up for the assembly. At the appropriate time during the demo we poured the chemicals and waited and waited and waited. We added more chemicals—stalled some more, looked at the reaction with a stink eye—no reaction. Then added more chemicals, no reaction.

Finally, after stalling for about 5 minutes, I set the experiment aside and went on with the other ideas. About 15 minutes later, between experiments, the whole tart pan burst into flames—and with all the extra chemicals it was quite a show. For every 10 degrees Celsius the rate of the reaction doubles. The lesson! Cold chemicals take a long time to react, warm ones will perform on command.

How Come, Huh?

As the glycerin (the clear liquid) is absorbed by the potassium permanganate (the purple powder), the molecules in the powder start to react with the molecules in the liquid. As the molecules split apart, they rapidly release the energy that held them together. This heat energy is enough to create a fire. If you watch carefully, you will see that the reaction spits little bombs as it proceeds.

Sewer Maggots

A Little Background

Gasses can be dissolved into liquids and that particular fact is experienced by some folks on a near daily basis. Carbon dioxide is the gas that is dissolved into soda pop liquid to give it the bubbly, fizzy appearance that you see when you pop the top off a bottle or can.

This lab also doubles as a lab on density. As the carbon dioxide adheres to the sides of raisins that are placed in the soft drink, they become buoyant and rise to the surface of the container. If they lose their carbon dioxide floats any time along the way, they become heavy and fall to the bottom again.

And finally, if you really want to have some fun, you can make up a story about sewer maggots, and totally gross out your friends. Inquiring minds want to know, and we will tell all.

Setting the Trap ...

I learned this lab years ago from a good friend and fellow college graduate, Dennis Bennett. Dennis took a position teaching school in a little town in Eastern Oregon. Calling it a rural area would be kind.

At any rate he had lots of time on his hands without the distractions of the big city so he invented his distractions—one of them being Sewer Maggots.

On the appointed day the kids would file into his classroom only to be greeted by a beaker sitting at the front of the room with a label that announced,

Sewer Maggots
Genetic Experiment
Caution!

OK, not your usual start to science class. He would then take roll, pour four cups of coffee and proceed to pound them, one after another. He would then explain what a diuretic compound did to the human kidneys, get a funny look on his face, and retire to the prep room.

Once there he would pour, as loudly as he could, Mountain Dew into a graduated cylinder. However, as far as the kids were concerned, he was engaged in another activity related to the rapid and copious ingestion of four cups of coffee.

In any event, he emerged triumphantly with a graduated cylinder full of a freshly acquired bright yellow-green liquid. Speculation was rampant.

Props

1	Can of Mountain Dew
1	Glass, 12 oz. or so
1	Box of raisins in a plastic tub
1	Cup of water, warm

The Zing!

1. Open the can of Mountain Dew and pour it into the glass. Mountain Dew, by design, is a yellowish liquid that could be easily presented as a sample of recently acquired sewer water. This is not to say that it tastes or in any other way resembles sewer water.

2. He would then announce to his students that here he had a sample of sewer water, and that he also wanted to introduce them to the insect community via a little critter called a "sewer maggot." The sewer maggot, he would explain, is used to purify the water. When sewer maggots are added to the sewer water, they can be seen diving up and down, gulping the various nutrients available. (At this point he would drop about 10 to 15 raisins, which had been soaking in warm water for about a half an hour, into the Mountain Dew, and they would start to bob up and down.)

Sewer Maggots

3. If you want to play this out a little bit more, you can explain that the sewer maggots swim around in the "pee" water and make it potable—a fancy word that means that you can drink it. To prove this to your friends take the container of "pee" water and sip it. Mmmm, mmmm, good—a little salty but good.

4. If they are not on the verge of tossing chunks yet, you can put them there by also telling them that maggots or larvae are a rich source of protein and considered delicacies in some areas of the world. Again, to prove this to them, catch a sewer maggot and pop it in your mouth and chew it up. You are now the pee-drinkin', maggot-munchin' kid who nobody is ever going to mess with.

MAGGOTS

SEWER WATER

5. Let your friends make observations, speculate, take measurements, but don't tell them what is really going on.

Things I've Screwed Up
Be sure to soak the raisin in warm water for at least 15 minutes. They plump up and float better than hard, dry raisins. You can also use dried cranberries and dried apricots that have been sliced up to give your maggot collection more color.

TOOBE

How Come, Huh?

This is more physics than it is chemistry. The bubbles of carbon dioxide stick to the sides of the raisins. When they do this, they decrease the average density of the raisin—the gas makes them less dense than the soda pop—and they float to the top of the container.

When the raisins get to the top, they start to roll and some of the gas is released. This makes the overall weight of the raisin heavier, and it starts to fall to the bottom of the container.

Take It & Run with It

2. The fizz that is present in all soda pop is called carbonation. The reason it has this name is that carbon dioxide—carbonic gas—is dissolved into the pop. Try the experiment with soda pop that has been sitting out for several hours and has had a chance to de-gas.

3. When you soaked the raisins in the warm water, they plumped up significantly and floated to the surface of the container quickly. Design an experiment where you try this procedure using raisins that have been soaked for different amounts of time in water.

Orange Sorbet Suds

A Little Background

This experiment is great for demonstrating volcanos, chemical reactions, expansion of gases, and it is always good for an "ooh, aah" from kids and adults like.

Baking soda and aluminum sulfate (the pickling spice alum) are mixed together with a little soap. The result is a pile of orange bubbles that look like a creamy, orange dessert.

Props

1   Pair of goggles
1   Pair of gloves
1   Toobe, or other container
1   Vial of sodium bicarbonate powder
1   1 oz. Bottle of yellow food coloring
1   Pie tin
1   Pre-form tube
1   Measuring cup
1   Vial of aluminum sulfate powder
1   1 oz. Bottle of detergent with squirt cap
1   1 oz. Bottle of red food coloring
1   #3 Solid stopper
1   Assistant
    Water

I CAP
BAKING SODA

1/3 TOOBE
WATER

The Zing!

1.   Have a friend help you with the following. Both of you should put on your gloves and goggles. Then fill the Toobe (a large acryllic cylinder), or other container, one-third full with water, add a cap of baking soda powder, add several drops of yellow food coloring, cover with the palm of your hand and shake like crazy. Place the Toobe in the center of the pie tin.

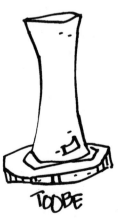

TOOBE

2. Add 2 ounces of water to the pre-form tube. Then add one cap of aluminum sulfate powder, one dash of detergent, and a couple of squirts of red food coloring. Stopper the pre-form tube and shake like crazy to mix the contents.

3. This is where you remind your assistant to be careful, and whatever you do, please don't make a mess.

Instruct him to quickly pour the aluminum sulfate solution into the Toobe and observe what happens.

4. A pile of orange foam will rise quickly up out of the Toobe and spill all over the table. Feign disgust, shock, disbelief, or anything that works.

How Come, Huh?

When you mix baking soda and aluminum sulfate in solution, they react with one another and release a gas called carbon dioxide. The gas forms a bubble and escapes to the top of the solution. The soap strengthens the solution and allows gas to be trapped.

Take It & Run with It

4. Make a big bowl of this stuff and set it in the dining room during one of the parties your folks have along with all of the other things to eat. Place some small paper bowls and plastic spoons nearby. Pick a spot to sit that has a good sight line as well as a quick exit from the room.

Chicken in a Cup

A Little Background

Sound is produced when an object vibrates. To take advantage of this idea and also tie it into a fun art project, we are going to show you how to make a chicken in a cup. This, in no way, is related to the chicken on a stick found in the taste lab section of another science book.

Setting the Trap ...

When your friends walk into the room, they will smell chicken soup. It is an unmistakable smell and an excellent way to set the stage. Inevitably they will ask you about the odor and you can explain that it is part of today's lab.

Inform them that scientists have figured out a way to distill down a chicken—in particular, their vocal cords—to an extract that will allow the sound of a chicken to be artificially reproduced upon command. At this point produce the beaker with a label on it that says, "Chicken Vocal Cord Extract, concentrated."

Explain that this technology may someday allow people who have lost their vocal cords to disease or injury to be able to speak again. Try to keep a straight face.

Props

1 Bouillon cube, chicken flavor
1 Cup
1 5 oz. Wax cup
1 Paper clip
1 12-inch Length of string
1 Pair of fingers
1 Piece of masking tape
   Water
1 250-ml Beaker
1 Roll of masking tape

The Zing!

1. Prepare a beaker full of chicken broth just before your friends come into the room.

2. Tell them that the delivery device for the vocal cord extract, called a Chicken Extract Amplifier, is very simple, and you will show them how to make one.

Open the paper clip up and punch a small hole in the center of the bottom of the wax cup. Put the end of the string over the hole and push it through to the other side using the paper clip. The idea is to keep the hole as small as possible so that more of the vibration is transferred to the cup and amplified.

3. Tie the paper clip to the outside end of the string. Reach into the cup and pull the string snug so that the paper clip is right on the bottom of the cup. Tape the paper clip to the bottom of the cup. Delivery device complete!

4. Grab the string with your thumb and forefinger near the bottom of the cup. Pull downward with short pulls and have the kids listen. Little-to-no sound should be produced, you are also demonstrating how to set up a control in an experiment—but let's not lose focus here.

5. Now wet the string with the chicken extract, soak it really well, and pull down on the string again using short, quick pulls. As your fingers move down the string, the unmistakable sound of a chicken clucking will be produced to the absolute amazement of your friends.

Chicken in a Cup

How Come, Huh?

The liquid on your fingers creates friction between your skin and the cotton string. As you move your fingers down the string, the string grabs your skin then is overcome by the downward force then grabs your skin again, which is overcome by the downward force, which grabs your skin, etc.

PULL DOWN

All of this stopping and starting along the string produces vibrations, which travel up the string. When they hit the bottom of the cup, it starts to vibrate too, and this is amplified by the shape of the cup. Good luck at the county fair!

Take It & Run with It

5. You can supersize this experiment. Take a 30-gallon garbage can, and attach a cotton rope to the bottom just like the mini version. Soak the rope in water and give it a tug. It sounds like a dinosaur with indigestion.

If you want to have some fun, take this to school, poke your head into the kindergarten class and tell the teacher that your pet dinosaur got loose. On cue have your friends pull the rope down the hall, and watch the eyes of those five-year-olds bug out.

Sound Carafe

A Little Background

You are going to heat a piece of metal alloy that has been folded and stuffed into one end of a large diameter steel tube. This will be heated with a propane torch. When the torch is removed from the bottom of the tube, it begins to hum. If you tilt the tube sideways, giving the illusion that you are "pouring" the sound out of the tube and into the second cup that you are holding, the sound will stop and appear to be collected in the cup. If you quickly tip the tube back into a vertical position and "pour" the sound that you collected in the second cup back into the top of the tube, the sound will appear to resume.

Setting the Trap ...

With a straight face, if that is possible, tell your friends that they will be observing a sound experiment today and will be introduced to other things like vibrations, frequency, pitch, amplitude, etc. They will also learn a little-known fact—sound has mass and can actually be poured from one container to another. Amazing, but true—or so it would appear.

Props

1   Oven mitt
1   Propane torch or Bunsen burner
1   Propane torch stand (optional)
1   Ignitor or book of matches
1   Steel tube, 19 inches x 1.5 inches
1   Metal alloy screen, 2 inches x 4 inches
1   Large, opaque, drinking glass
    Adult Supervision

The Zing!

1. Insert the screen two inches up into either end of the metal tube. Fire up the torch and put the oven mitt on the hand that is going to hold the tube.

Sound Carafe

2. The key to this experiment is to get the screen inside the bottom of the tube red hot using the torch. To achieve that end, you are going to want to hold the tube upright with the metal alloy screen toward the end nearest the torch.

3. Insert the flame of the torch into the bottom of the tube so that it is heating the alloy screen directly. When the screen gets hot enough, the tube will begin to hum _but not until you remove the flame from inside the tube_. This usually takes about 15 to 20 seconds. Every tube is different so it would be a good idea to practice and time your particular tube before you uncork this one on your family and friends.

4. The screen is hot enough, the tube starts to hum, eyeballs bug out and kids are really impressed. Don't stop now; it's zinger time. Pick up the large, opaque, plastic cup—the 44-oz. kind they sell at convenience stores works great. Hold the cup up and tilt the tube at an angle so that it looks like you are literally "pouring" the sound from the tube into the cup. The interesting thing is that as soon as you tip the tube over the sound ceases. Quickly return the tube to its upright position and "pour" the sound back into the tube from the cup, and it will start to hum again.

How Come, Huh?

Touch a propane torch to anything and it's a sure bet that it is going to get hot. As the hot screen heats the air inside the tube, a convection current starts to form and the air rises through the tube. The air escaping from the top of the tube creates an area of low pressure just above the screen, and cold air enters the bottom of the tube. As it passes through the hot screen, it is heated rapidly and starts to rise turbulently through the tube. This turbulent motion produces a wave of vibrating air molecules that our ears interpret as a hum.

When you tip the tube sideways, you disrupt the movement of the air. Because air molecules don't get a chance to bounce around inside the tube and produce the vibrations, the sound ceases. By returning the tube to its vertical position, the air is free to rise and produce sound again. For the record, you cannot pour sound. It's an illusion. That is, if it is well done, and that's where the practice comes in.

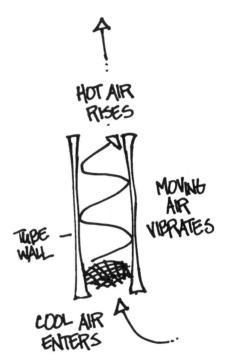

Take It & Run with It

6. Experiment with different lengths and diameters of tubes. You will be able to produce all kinds of sounds.

pH Pandemonium

A Little Background

A blue chemical indicator called bromothymol blue is added to a large Toobe with water in it. A piece of dry ice (solid carbon dioxide) is added to the tube. As the ice hits the water, you immediately start to see the gas sublimating off the surface. It produces bubbles that rise to the surface, immediately condense the warm air, and produce fog.

All the while that this is happening the liquid in the tube turns from blue to sea green to a light yellow color in a matter of seconds. When the reaction has proceeded to the yellow phase, you add a couple of drops of dilute sodium hydroxide and the whole glass turns back to blue and starts over again. Sublimation, pH, and chemical indicators all introduced in one fell swoop.

Setting the Trap ...

Have a large tube full of water sitting on the table where it is easily visible. Tell your friends that you have a piece of dry ice, solid carbon dioxide, and you are going to demonstrate several of the properties it possesses. One, it can produce fog, two it can change liquids different colors, and three it acts as a cannon.

Props

- 2   Toobes, or other containers
  Gloves (for dry ice)
- 1   Piece of dry ice, 2 oz. to 4 oz.
- 1   Bottle of bromothymol blue
- 1   Bottle of sodium hydroxide
  (10% solution)
- 1   Pipette
- 1   Stopper, solid, #12
  Water
  Adult Supervision

The Zing!

1. Dry ice is solid carbon dioxide, and if you could take its temperature, you would find that it is 112 degrees below zero. Very cold. So cold that if you were to pick the dry ice up with your fingers and hold it for more than a couple of seconds, you would get what is called a cold burn. The cells in your fingers would freeze solid, die, and then turn black. Pretty.

DRY ICE

TOOBE
WITH WATER

2. Fill one Toobe, or other container, three-fourths full of water. Glove up and drop a Ping-Pong ball–sized chunk of dry ice into the Toobe. It will immediately begin producing white bubbles that rise to the surface of the water and burst into fog.

3. Let your friends observe this for about a minute. Not only is it entertaining but also you are acidifying the water with the carbon dioxide, which is important for the next step.

Tell them that this solution will also turn a blue compound yellow almost instantly. Hold up the bottle of bromothymol blue so the kids can see the color. Add a dash of bromothymol blue to your bubbling tube. The indicator will turn yellow almost immediately.

4. Once the solution has turned a light yellow, pour the liquid contents into the second Toobe; leave the dry ice in the first Toobe. Tell the kids that the blue solution that turned yellow is actually neither color. It is green.

Take the pipette and fill it with sodium hydroxide. Carefully add a drop at a time. You will notice that as you near a pH of 7.0, the color starts to become sea green. Add one or two more drops and stir the tube. If you hit the pH perfectly, you will have a tube full of green liquid.

pH Pandemonium

5. Finally, pour the green liquid back into the tube with the dry ice and stopper it. As the gas pressure inside the tube builds, it will push on the stopper. When it gets high enough, it will shoot the stopper into the air. Voila! You have a color-changing cannon and all of the associated pandemonium to go with it.

Things I've Screwed Up

1. If you add too much base (sodium hydroxide), you will zip right past the green color and the solution will turn blue. Entertaining but it doesn't follow the story line. Go slowly and stir after each drop.

2. When it comes time to insert the stopper, only add enough water to fill the Toobe two-thirds full. You want to have some room for the gas to accumulate and build up pressure. If it is too full, the stopper will shoot, but it will not be as dramatic.

How Come, Huh?

Bromothymol blue, also known as dibromothymolsulfon-phthalein, is an acid base indicator that operates in a pH range of 6.0 to 7.6. When it is in a basic solution, it exhibits a blue color; when neutral, it is green; and when slightly acidic, it is yellow. As the piece of dry ice sublimates to gas, the carbon dioxide acidifies the water. The more carbon dioxide that bubbles through the water, the lower the pH gets. When it reaches a neutral level, it turns green; and when it becomes acidic, it turns yellow. When the sodium hydroxide is added (a couple of drops at a time), this base causes the pH to rise again. The solution turns back to blue and starts over again.

Take It & Run with It

7. The are 25 or 30 different chemical indicators. Grab a Merck index and try other indicators for other color sequences.

Eggzasperating Puzzle

A Little Background

Three containers, three clear liquids, three eggs—all we need now are the Three Stooges, but alas, they have all retired to the Big Lab in the Sky so we'll have to wing it.

This lab addresses density. You are going to take three identical containers, fill them with three liquids, and place a fresh egg in each container. Despite apparent similarities in these conditions, the egg in the first container sinks right to the bottom. The egg in the second container is not interested in sinking at all, and instead, it floats right on top of the liquid. The third egg, truly an individual, decides to neither sink or float but simply hover in the middle? Density weirdness is alive and well.

Setting the Trap ...

Show the three eggs to your friends and tell them that the eggs came from three different chickens who have been on three different diets: high fat, low fat, and regular. This, of course, is not true, but your intention is to head them down the wrong road at the outset. Tell them that you are going to put the eggs into three identical containers (not liquids, containers) of identical volume, and it is their job to guess which chicken produced which egg.

Eggzasperating Puzzle

Props

3   500-ml Beakers
1   Pound of salt
1   Spoon
3   Eggs, fresh
     Water

The Zing!

1. Before anyone arrives, fill beaker number 1 full of water. That's it, not too glamorous—keep going.

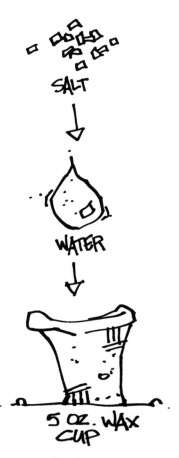

2. Fill beaker number 2 <u>half</u> full of water and add four heaping spoons of salt. Stir the solution until all of the salt dissolves.

Fill the container full of water and continue dissolving the remaining salt. If you use warm water, you will find that the dissolving of the salt goes a little faster.

3. Fill beaker number 3 <u>half</u> full of water and add four heaping spoons of salt. Once again, stir the container until all of the salt dissolves.

Place the spoon inside the glass or Toobe and slowly pour water into the container on top of the layer of salt water. As the water level rises, lift the spoon up also to minimize the mixing of the fresh water with the salt water. Fill the container all the way to the top.

4. With your audience present, add an egg to each container. The best way to do this is to place the egg in the spoon and lower the spoon into the liquid, rolling the egg out of the spoon gently.

5. Here is where you get to freelance a bit. Start a discussion about which egg could come from the low-fat chicken and why. Encourage them to speculate, ask questions, and develop tests on the spot. Let them continue to speculate, discuss, and argue until they find out what is really going on.

Things I've Screwed Up

1. The eggs need to be fresh. It is tempting to take those old, unused, hard-boiled eggs out of the fridge and recycle them during lab time, but you will not get the desired result.

2. I thought I would be cute and get three different eggs— white, brown, and speckled—to make the presentation even more believeable, but not all chicken eggs are created equal. Get three white ones, and let the imaginations do the rest.

How Come, Huh?

All liquids produce what is called a buoyant force. It is the force of the molecules in the liquid that push up on a foreign body that is in the liquid. When you added salt to the water, you increased the buoyant force of the liquid.

Here's what happened in each case. Beaker number 1 contained fresh water. The weight of the egg was greater than the buoyant force of the water so the egg sank. In beaker number 2, the salt increased the buoyant force of the water significantly, so much so that the weight of the egg was supported by the liquid.

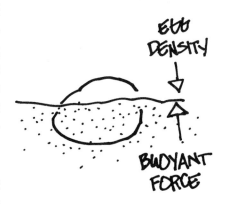

EGG DENSITY

BUOYANT FORCE

Beaker number 3 is your sneaker. The weight of the egg was

Eggzasperating Puzzle

too great for the buoyant force of the fresh water in the top half of the beaker. When the egg sank far enough to encounter the salt water layer, it stopped sinking because the buoyant force at that point in the solution was great enough to support it.

Take It & Run with It

8. You can repeat the experiment and get a little more sophisticated by incorporating additional containers. Vary the ratios of the salt water to fresh water. Set the lab up before your friends come to see it, and you can have five different containers with eggs floating all the way from the top to the bottom and four different places in-between. Drives 'em crazy.

9. Place two different cans of soda pop in a tub of water. One can is regular soda pop and the other, diet. One will float, one will sink—answers please. Experiment with different brands of soda and diet soda pop. Try regular cola, root beer, lemon lime, and the diet versions of the same drink. Graph your results.

Dancing Bubbles

A Little Background

Soap bubbles are blown into the air over an aquarium. They snake some hang time, but eventually gravity gets the best of the situation and the bubbles are pulled down into the aquarium full of dry ice. The funny thing is that they do not sink to the bottom of the aquarium, but instead, they mysteriously float and bounce in the middle of the tank, supported by a gas that is much denser than air.

Your task, should you assume the responsibility for this investigation, is to determine why the bubbles did not sink to the bottom of the container—and where did the gas come from in the first place? A classic investigation into the density of gases if there ever was one.

Props

1   Pair of gloves, cotton
1   Pound of dry ice
1   Cloth or paper bag
1   Hammer
1   10-gallon Aquarium
1   Bottle of bubble solution with wand
1   1-gallon Plastic bucket
Adult Supervision

The Zing!

Warning! *Dry ice is 109 degrees Fahrenheit below zero. If you touch it with bare hands, you run the risk of freezing the skin cells solid, which tends to kill them instantly. Be safe and use the gloves. You will avoid a lot of pain and the unsightly appearance of greenish-black fingers.*

Dancing Bubbles

1. Set the dry ice on a hard surface. Cover it with a cloth or insert it in a paper bag, and smash it into little pieces with the hammer. Again, with gloved hands, either empty the pieces of dry ice directly from the bag into the aquarium or remove the cover, pick up the dry ice pieces, and place them in the aquarium.

2. Allow the dry ice pieces to stand undisturbed in the bottom of the aquarium for a couple of minutes. Dry ice is the solid form of carbon dioxide. At room temperature, dry ice undergoes a process called *sublimation,* changing directly from a solid to a gas. As you wait, the aquarium will fill up with this invisible carbon dioxide gas. Because carbon dioxide is heavier than air, it displaces, or pushes the air up and out of the aquarium.

3. After two or three minutes, take the bubble solution and blow bubbles *over* the top of the aquarium so that they float down into it. Do not blow down into the aquarium, or you will blow the gas out of the container. Observe the bubbles. This is where they get weird. The carbon dioxide in the tank is heavier than the air trapped in the bubbles, so they look like spheres bobbing up and down on an invisible ocean of gas—which, curiously enough, is exactly what is happening.

4. Fill the aquarium with bubbles, and then gently tilt it at a 45-degree angle. The bubbles will "ride" the heavier carbon dioxide gas out of the aquarium and onto the floor.

5. Allow the gas to accumulate in the aquarium again and then blow more bubbles. When you have 10 to 15 bubbles floating on the layer of carbon dioxide, gently tip the aquarium back and forth. As the carbon dioxide sloshes back and forth, the motion of the gas will be recorded in the movement of the bubbles on the surface of the gas.

6. Take a bucket and wearing gloves, place a couple of pieces of dry ice in the bucket, and then pour the gas from the bucket into the aquarium when there are bubbles floating on the surface. As the level of carbon dioxide increases, the height of the bubbles inside the container will get higher and higher.

How Come, Huh?

Dry ice is solid carbon dioxide, a substance that is usually a gas at room temperature. When the dry ice is placed in the tank, it sublimes, which means that it changes directly from a solid to a gas without ever becoming a liquid. As the dry ice changes to a gas (one that is heavier than air, we might add), it starts to fill the tank. Remember that two chunks of matter can't occupy the same space? Same deal here. The carbon dioxide is heavier, so it pushes the lighter air out of the tank. Check out the illustrations to the right.

Dancing Bubbles

When the bubbles—full of air—fall into the aquarium, they stop when they hit the layer of heavier carbon dioxide—just like tossing a piece of wood on the water. It just floats. The bubbles look like they are floating because the gas inside the tank behaves like a liquid and is moving constantly.

OXYGEN
MOLECULE
(O_2)

Take It & Run with It

10. You can demonstrate the density of the gas—carbon dioxide—and the role of oxygen in combustion at the same time. With adult supervision, light a votive candle and place it on the edge of the aquarium. Take an empty glass and fill it full of carbon dioxide by scooping it into the aquarium. Gently pour the carbon dioxide directly from the cup onto the flame of the candle, which will extinguish immediately.

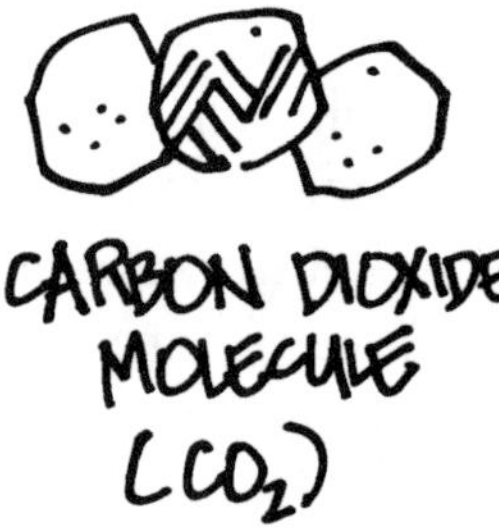

CARBON DIOXIDE
MOLECULE
(CO_2)

11. Set up a relay competition where carbon dioxide gas is ferried from a main source to an outpost. First one to get the bubbles to overflow is the winner.

Magnetic Fingers

A Little Background

A 2-liter pop bottle is filled almost to overflowing with water. An eyedropper is placed on the surface of the water where it floats. When you place your hands on the sides of the bottle and squeeze, the eyedropper sinks to the bottom of the jug; when you release the sides, the eyedropper rises again. Pretty much the same way that submarines works only you don't have to squeeze them on the sides. Density, pressure, and states of matter all conspiring to provide you an education.

Setting the Trap ...

The best way to set this up is to magnetize nails a couple of days before this demo. You take a bar magnet, rub it on the nail and demonstrate how the magnetism can be induced. This provides your mind set.

Tell the kids that not only can you magnetize a nail, but you can also magnetize a finger. Why, because there is blood flowing through it and everyone knows that a major component of blood is iron. The same kind of iron that was in the nail that you magnetized.

It gets better. Not only can you magnetize a finger but also that magnetized finger can attract a glass and rubber eyedropper …

Props

1   Empty 2-liter pop bottle
     Water
1   Eyedropper
1   Drinking glass
1   Bar magnet
1   Volunteer

Magnetic Fingers

The Zing!

1. Fill the pop bottle almost all the way to the top with water.

2. Remove the rubber bulb from the top of the eyedropper and dunk it into a glass full of water. As you do this, you will notice that the dropper fills with water. Without removing the dropper, place the rubber bulb back on the eyedropper. This traps the water inside the dropper. Remove the dropper from the water and squeeze the bulb gently, forcing water out of the bulb so that it is roughly two-thirds full.

BULB

WATER — LEVEL

EYEDROPPER

3. Place the diver (eyedropper) in the pop bottle and screw the cap on tightly. If the diver gets to the bottom of the jug but does not return to the surface, retrieve it by first emptying the jug to retrieve the dropper and then squeezing some of the water out of the eyedropper. Refill the jug and try again. If you attempt to sink the diver but it won't go, try adding a little more water to the dropper. When you are all set to experiment, it will look like the illustration at the right.

4. Place the eyedropper in the pop bottle and ask your friends to observe what you have set up. Ask a volunteer to come up and hold his finger next to the bottle, near the eyedropper. On your instruction he is to move his finger down the side of the bottle to test and see if his finger is magnetized. Nothing should happen, the eyedropper will remain at the top of the bottle.

5. Take the bar magnet and magnetize his finger the same way that you would magnetize nails. A single stroke, lift; stroke, lift; line up the iron particles in the blood, lift; induce the magnetic field, lift, and stroke about 20 times.

6. This time when he puts his finger next to the bottle, you will be ready to squeeze the bottle. Use the illustration above to see how you should hold it. As your volunteer moves his finger slowly down the side of the bottle, you start to subtly squeeze the sides. The pressure on the bottle causes the dropper to start to sink slowly.

7. Ask your volunteer to stop mid-bottle. If you hold the pressure just right, you will suspend the eyedropper right in the middle of the bottle. Go back up, then back down, always using pressure to control the location and speed of the eyedropper. The kids will be absolutely amazed.

Magnetic Fingers

Things I've Screwed Up

1. Be sure that your eyedropper is properly set up. This demo gets screwed up faster with an eyedropper that is not balanced than anything else.

2. Use a clear bottle rather than a green one—it is easier for the kids in the cheap seats to see what is going on.

How Come, Huh?

When you placed your hands on the bottle and squeezed, the pressure inside the jug increased. You were squeezing the water molecules together, and they began to look for a place to go to release that pressure. Since liquids do not compress as easily as gases, the air in the eyedropper was mooshed together and more water went into the eyedropper. The added weight of the water inside the eyedropper caused it to sink. When the pressure was released, the water came out and the eyedropper became buoyant enough to rise to the surface again.

Take It & Run with It

12. Supersize it up to 3 liters.

The Despanding Balloon

A Little Background

Pardon the word *despanding*. It was created by my three-year-old daughter who watched me do the experiment and then in her excitement was trying her very best to explain it to her mother.

This particular experiment demonstrates several ideas. First of all it reinforces the idea that air is matter and matter takes up space. Second, if there is a difference in air pressure, that difference is sometimes great enough to create a significant amount of force. And, third, not only does nature abhore a vacuum, but also trying to work against one is a pain in the fanny.

Setting the Trap ...

Most folks learn that heat causes solids, liquids, and gases to expand. The molecules need more space to move around when they get hot. Makes sense. However, this does not always hold true. Rubber, for example, actually shrinks when it is heated and to demonstrate this anomaly of physics all you need is a rubber water balloon, a wide-mouth jar, and matches.

Props

1	Rubber balloon, round
	Water
1	1-gallon, Wide-mouth jar
2	Paper towels
1	Book of matches
1	Drinking straw, plastic
1	Pair of goggles
	Adult Supervision

The Zing!

1. Make a water balloon that is about one and a half times the size of the opening of the mouth of the jar and tie it off. It should be the size of a very large grapefruit. Goggle up.

The Despanding Balloon

2. Place the jar on a hard, level surface and put the water balloon on the mouth of the jar. It should be quite a bit larger than the opening of the jar. Now, push down on the balloon from the top, try your best to shove the balloon into the jar. You may not squeeze the balloon or wiggle it down in by pushing on the sides—just push from the top.

You should notice that this is a bit tough and despite your best efforts the balloon simply squished out to the sides. Obviously too big to fit in the jar—unless you can find some way to get the balloon to contract.

3. Remove the balloon, and with adult supervision, light a paper towel on fire with the matches, and drop it inside the jar. When you are sure that it is burning well, replace the water balloon on the opening of the jar. The balloon may bounce up and down a couple of times and then will definitely disappear into the jar.

4. At this point you have proven your point. The fire in the jar caused the balloon to shrink, the skinny balloon fell into the jar, once again you have bequeathed new and innovative concepts to the minds of unsuspecting victims.

5. Now try to pull the balloon out of the jar. Grab the knot that you tied and pull straight up. If you have trouble, you are in good company—kids all over the world have tried this and they were unsuccessful. In fact, if you are careful, you can lift the balloon up and the jar will come with it, like the cartoon to the right. Use caution when you do this.

6. To get the balloon out of the jar take a straw and hold it inside the jar next to the edge of the mouth. Using your other hand, pull the balloon up to the mouth trapping the straw against the side of the jar. To remove the balloon simply give it a quick tug and the balloon and the straw will both pop up out of the jar.

7. Which is great but it shoots a huge hole in your shrinking balloon theory. Turn your friends loose and see if they can figure out what is going on.

Things I've Screwed Up

Have a back-up balloon ready. I would say that about one out of fifty times something happens and the balloon explodes. The audience loves it, it is very funny, but it is alway nice to have a back-up balloon ready to go.

The Despanding Balloon

How Come, Huh?

A. When you placed the balloon on the mouth of the jar, you were trapping a jar full of air. Air is matter and takes up space. As you pushed on the balloon, it wouldn't go into the jar because the air in the jar was pushing back up on the balloon—there was no room for the balloon. The jar was full. As you push, the air inside the jar compresses slightly but not enough to allow the balloon to enter the jar.

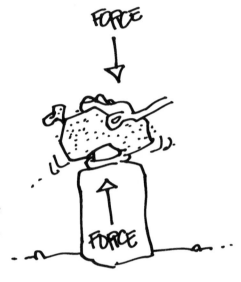

This is another demonstration that there is air and air does take up space, and this is illustrated by the cartoon to the right. You can see that the force on top of the bottle balances out the force inside the bottle created by the air. The end result is no movement.

B. When you placed the burning paper into the jar, two different opposing actions began to take place. First, the fire began to heat the air inside, which caused it to expand. These expanding air molecules created pressure inside the bottle that was not there earlier, and they don't like this so they try to find a way out of the jar. Fortunately the balloon is resting on the top of the jar and is acting like a one-way valve.

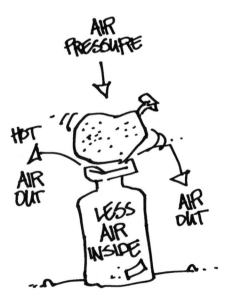

As the air continues to heat and expand, the pressure inside the jar continues to build up until it is strong enough to push the balloon up—this is like opening a valve just enough to let out a burp of air from inside the jar. Once the air escapes, the pressure is lowered inside so that the balloon once again seals off the container. This pushing action can occur several times in rapid succession in a very short period of time. This makes the balloon look like it is dancing on top of the jar.

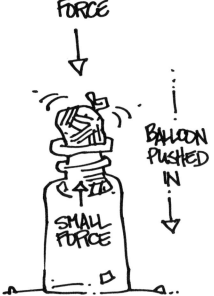

The other thing that is going on is the oxidation, or burning, of oxygen. As the paper towel burned inside the jar, some of the oxygen in it was changed from a gas state to a solid state. Solids take up much less space than gases, about 1800 time less, and this means that the pressure inside the jar is reduced. Low pressure inside, higher pressure outside, and the balloon gets pushed into the jar. Use the illustration to help you out if you are stuck understanding this idea, but whatever you do remember that the balloon was pushed into the jar and not sucked.

The Despanding Balloon

C. In the last portion of the experiment when you were trying to get the balloon back out of the jar, you had air pressure working against you. As you pulled the balloon to the top of the jar, the air inside the jar is once again trapped behind the balloon—just like when you put the balloon on the top of the jar. The moment this happens there is a balance of forces both inside and out. The air pressure inside the jar is equal to the air pressure outside the jar. The balloon likes this and is not going to go anywhere when this occurs. If you try to pull the balloon up, you begin to create lower pressure inside the jar and the balloon is pushed back inside by the atmosphere. When you inserted the straw, you allowed air to rush by the balloon and down into the jar to replace the space left by the balloon as it was being pulled up and out of the jar. If the air can get into the jar through the straw, the forces never get a chance to balance and the balloon can be pulled from the jar very easily.

Ice-Cube Roundup

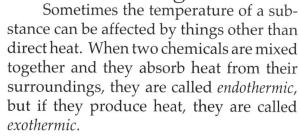

A Little Background

Sometimes the temperature of a substance can be affected by things other than direct heat. When two chemicals are mixed together and they absorb heat from their surroundings, they are called *endothermic*, but if they produce heat, they are called *exothermic*.

In this lab, salt will be added to water, lowering the temperature and ultimately causing it to refreeze. We are going to take advantage of this reaction to capture a couple of wayward ice cubes. Using nothing more than a piece of cotton string and a little chemistry chutzpah.

Setting the Trap ...

You can do this lab as a demo, but it is also a great problem solver to give to your friends and let them noodle away on it for a while. If you have a Toobe, toss a couple of ice cubes down into the bottom and ask your buds to rescue the cubes using just a piece of string. A couple of rules, 1) the Toobe must remain upright and vertical at all times—no tipping, 2) the only solid, physical object you can use is a string, 3) if the ice cube melts before you are finished, you lose.

Props

1   Ice cube
1   Length of string
1   Packet of salt
1   5-inch Diameter pie tin
      or
1   Toobe or other container

Ice-Cube Round Up

The Zing!

1. Rinse the ice cube under the water for just a second and then place it in the pie tin or Toobe. Place the string directly on top of the ice cube. Do your very best to catch it. Wrap it under, around, speak with it sternly if you must, but no touching the cube with your fingers or any other solid object.

2. When your frustration level is tapped out, open the salt packet, lay the string across the top of the ice cube, and sprinkle a little bit of salt over the surface of the ice cube. Be sure to sprinkle salt on the string as well.

3. Count to five and lift the loose end of the string—and you too can be an accomplished ice-cube fisherman.

4. Once you have caught one ice cube, go for the record. Lay as many ice cubes together as your supply will allow. Then wiggle the string in, around, and through the assortment, and salt the entire collection. As you do this, you may want to be careful when you salt—some folks have a special ability to get the ice cubes to freeze to the pie tin or Toobe.

5. As your string of ice cubes grows, see if you can get ice cubes that you have already caught to catch other ice cubes even without the string coming in direct contact.

SALT

COTTON STRING

ICE CUBE

Things I've Screwed Up

There are two things that mess this lab up, 1) you can put too much salt on the string, and 2) you can be too messy and get salt all over the bottom of the Toobe or pan, freezing the ice cube to the container.

How Come, Huh?

As the ice cube sits at room temperature, it begins to melt, and a layer of water is formed on the surface of the cube. When you place the string on the ice cube, nothing happens, but it does get slightly wet in the water layer.

Sprinkling salt on the string and the ice cube causes the salt to dissolve in the thin layer of water on the surface of the cube. When the salt atoms break apart (dissolve), the process takes heat away from the water on the surface of the ice cube and in the string, lowering the temperature. When the salt water moves away from the string, the fresh water, exposed to lower temperatures refreezes, connecting the string to the ice cube. All of this results in a successful ice-cube roundup.

Take It & Run with It

13. This is not so much an extension of science as a fun activity that you can do with your friends—have an ice-cube relay. Give each kid a cotton string and line them up in two lines at one end of the competition area. Have a pile of ice cubes at the other end. When the starter says, "Go," the kids race down to the pile of ice cubes, line up and salt as many of them as possible, and race back to the line. The team with the most ice cubes wins.

Water Slide

A Little Background

Water molecules are incredibly good at hanging onto one another. The reason for this is that it is a bipolar molecule. Fancy word? Maybe, but easy to understand. *Bi* means two, and *polar* refers to the poles or ends of a magnet where the magnetic field is strongest. So a water molecule is actually a little magnet with a positive end and negative end. Put two or more in a container and they are attracted to one another.

This arrangement gives water some unique characteristics that produce effects like surface tension, capillary action, and cohesion—which will be demonstrated in this lab activity. We are going to start with cohesion—a term that could be defined as "sticky." You are going to fill a clean, empty soup can with water and pour that water, along a cotton string, down to another soup can without spilling any water.

Setting the Trap ...

Hand a soup can full of water to your friend who is about 10 feet from you. Tell her that you would like a drink of water but show her your can, which is empty. Her task is to figure out a way to get the water from her seat to you. Here are the conditions:

A. She cannot leave her chair.
B. She cannot pass the can to anyone else in the room
C. She must not spill any water.
D. The can cannot leave her hand.

Props

2   #303 Soup cans
1   Cotton string, 12 feet long
    Water
1   Friend
1   Chair

The Zing!

1.   After you have had a sufficient number of suggestions, assuming that no one knows the answer, pass a 12-foot long piece of thick, cotton string to your friend with the water.

2.   Instruct her to dip the entire piece of cotton string into the water and get it soaking wet. Have her toss you one end of the soaking wet string.

3.   Using the illustration below showing how to do this by yourself as a magic trick, stretch the string from one can to the other. Make sure the ends are inside the cans.

4. For this experiment to work the can full of water must be higher than the empty can. Ask your volunteer to stand on her chair and, keeping the ends of the strings in place with her fingers, tip the can just a bit to start a stream of water trickling down the string.

Water Slide

5. As the can empties, have her tip it just a bit more and the water will continue to flow until she has emptied the top can and filled the bottom can. Again, patience is the key to this experiment. A constant and steady trickle of water is best.

How Come, Huh?

The illustrations to the right should help a lot. A water molecule is made up of three atoms, two hydrogens and one oxygen. The two hydrogen atoms sit on top of the oxygen atom and create a positive charge on that end of the molecule. This also exposes the oxygen atom, which has a negative charge. With positive charges on one end and negative on the other, you have a little, tiny magnet.

The cotton string absorbed the water when it was dunked in the can. As the water from the can started to trickle out onto the string the water molecules in the string were attracted to the water molecules sliding down the string. Another word for this attraction is *cohesion*. Gravity pulled the water drop along the string, but the cohesion kept it from falling to the floor.

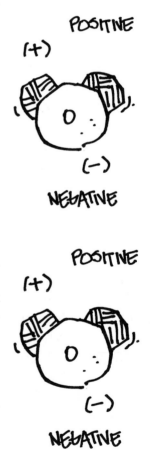

POSITIVE
(+)

(−)
NEGATIVE

POSITIVE
(+)

(−)
NEGATIVE

Take It & Run with It

14. Try other kinds of transport media like fishing line, steel wire, guitar strings, fabric strips, and compare your results.

Magnetic Bubbles

A Little Background

A rubber balloon will be rubbed on someone's head, preferably with shoulder-length, fine hair, but any pile of clean hair will work. The rubbing action collects free electrons from the surface of the hair. As these electrons pile up on the surface of the balloon, the hair shafts will begin to float and repel one another.

You can stick this charged balloon to the ceiling, walls, passing dogs, or wool sweaters. However, the point of this lab is to explore the electrostatic effect of an accumulated charge on a soap bubble. A soap bubble simply being a drip of water that got stretched out into a sphere.

Setting the Trap ...

Invite that proverbial, unsuspecting friend to help you with this experiment and ask her if she happened to bring her electrons with her today. Depending on many factors, the responses will range from trying to explain to you that she did, to looking at you with a freshly lobotomized stare.

Work through the response and announce that you are going to steal some of her electrons to make a magnet with them, using a balloon. More stares. Continue that this balloon will attract soap bubbles that are blown into the room by the electron donor. Lobotomies for everyone!

Props

1   Rubber balloon, round, 9 inch
1   Person, full head of hair
1   Bottle of bubble solution

Magnetic Bubbles

The Zing!

Before we start, it is important to note that this experiment—like all electrostatic experiments—works best in low humidity.

1. Inflate the balloon and tie it off.

2. Hopefully you have pre-selected your volunteer. For best results use someone who has shoulder-length hair that is free of mousse, hair spray, or gel. Fine hair tends to work better than coarse hair—and remember, blondes may have more fun, but not until you rub their heads with a rubber balloon.

3. Rub the balloon back and forth all over the hair. As you rub, occasionally lift the balloon up off her hair about 6 inches. Her hair will follow.

After about 30 seconds of rubbing, the hair strands should be positively charged, which causes them to be sticking up and floating all around the place. Kind of a sea urchin effect without the sea urchin or the water.

4. Ask your volunteer to take the cap off the bubble solution and blow several bubbles *up* into the air. Hold the charged balloon just a couple of inches above the soap bubbles, and you will find that several of them will be attracted toward the balloon. As the bubbles rise toward the balloon, you have to be careful to keep the balloon moving away or the bubble will zip right into the balloon and explode on the surface.

5. Select one bubble and practice bringing the balloon close to it. Get so that you can tug the bubble all over the room with the balloon. As long as you keep a safe distance, you will have a very obedient bubble.

Things I've Screwed Up

Practice attracting the bubbles. The closer the bubble gets to the balloon, the more likely it will accelerate into and explode on the balloon. In addition to making your balloon sticky it also reverses the polarity of the balloon—but that's another whole lab.

How Come, Huh?

Opposite charges (negative and positive) attract, and like charges (negative and negative) or (positive and positive) repel. It's the same way with magnets. The balloon has a huge negative charge because it has stolen all the loose electrons from the hair shafts, and the hair has a huge positive charge because all of its electrons have been stolen. Balloon negative, hair positive: They attract. When you take the balloon out of the picture, the hair still tends to stand up on end. This is because each of the hair strands has a positive charge. Like charges repel, and since they can't stand each other, they get as far away from one another as is possible. In this case they stand on end.

The bubble is attracted to the static charge on the balloon because our water molecule has one side that is positively charged and one side that is negatively charged. Opposites attract.

Take It & Run with It

15. Bubbles are attracted to things with a large negative charge. Give yourself a charge with a Van de Graaff generator and enjoy!

One-Way Cheesecloth

A Little Background

If you take a piece of cheesecloth and hold it up to the light, you will see thousands of little holes. Despite the fact that there are all of these holes, cheesecloth makes a very effective lid for a container of water—weird but true.

This lab will allow you to explore surface tension—the ability of water molecules to hang onto one another, in small spaces. In this case you are going to explore the characteristics of cheesecloth and try to explain the fact that water can flow freely through cheesecloth in one direction but not in the other.

Setting the Trap ...

Hold up a chunk of cheesecloth and show the kids all the holes in it. Explain that this particular kind of cheesecloth has an interesting characteristic in that water can flow through one side of the cloth but will not flow the other way.

Props

1   Toobe or other container
1   Cheesecloth, 6 inches by 6 inches square
1   Rubber band
1   Drinking glass, 10 to 12 oz.
    Water

The Zing!

1. Starting with an empty Toobe, or other container, place the twice folded cheesecloth over the opening, pull it tight, and put a rubber band over it to hold it in place.

2. Fill the drinking glass with water and pour it directly into the Toobe from a height of about 10 inches. You will notice that you have no trouble filling your Toobe with water. Use the illustration to the left as a guide.

3. Now for the reverse reaction. Holding your Toobe over a sink or outside where you can make a mess, quickly flip it upside down with your hand on top of the cheesecloth. Slowly remove your hand and observe what happens to the water in the Toobe.

4. Flip the Toobe over again, and this time when you invert it, you will not need to use your hand to support the cheesecloth, provided that you flip the whole contraption quickly enough. The Toobe is now upright.

5. Flip the Toobe back and forth several times and ask your friends to speculate why the water can be poured into the Toobe, but with the Toobe upside down, the water does not fall out of the Toobe. Take their suggestions and see if you can come to some sort of conclusion about what is going on here.

One-Way Cheesecloth

Things I've Screwed Up

Make sure the cheesecloth has a chance to get wet and the holes are filled with water before you remove your hand. It does not take long, but if you flip it over and the cloth is dry, some of the water will spill out.

How Come, Huh?

When you are pouring the water into the Toobe, it has lots of energy. Starting out 10 inches above the Toobe gives it lots of potential energy. As the water is pulled by gravity toward the Toobe, it speeds up and has even more energy, so that when it hits the holes in the cheesecloth, it zips right on through and into the bottom of the container. That explains the first half of the experiment.

A couple of things happen in the second part of the experiment. First, as you flip the Toobe upside down, your hand temporarily blocks the water from falling by holding it inside the container. This gives the water time to clog the holes in the cheesecloth, which it does because of that natural attraction between water molecules—it's that magnet thing. So the water molecules are hanging onto each other, plugging the holes in the cheesecloth. But we still don't know why the water doesn't come gushing out of the Toobe when you remove your hand. This is because when you flip the Toobe upside down, you are actually creating a partial vacuum at the top of the Toobe.

So here's the scenario: Water is plugging the holes of the cheesecloth, which basically makes a single uniform surface. A couple of pounds of water and a little bit of air pressure inside the Toobe are pushing *down* on the cheesecloth; 14.7 pounds per square inch of air pressure are pushing *up* on the cheesecloth. The water does not have enough weight or energy to push the cheesecloth out of the way so that it can escape— hence a one-way cheesecloth.

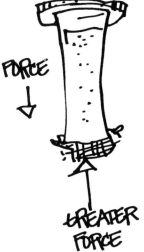

FORCE

GREATER FORCE

Take It & Run with It

16. Repeat this experiment using an index card, sheet of cardboard, piece of aluminum foil, or other surface of your choice in place of the cheesecloth and see if you can replicate the results.

17. Repeat this experiment using a dry piece of cheesecloth, but this time when you flip the whole concoction over, do not place your hand over the opening at first. Explain your results.

18. Try other kinds of materials—cotton, silk, rayon, burlap— and see if you can duplicate the results that you got with the cheesecloth. Compare the size of the holes in the fabric with the effectiveness of the fabric as a cloth and try to determine if that has anything at all to do with this experiment.

The Instant Bubbler

A Little Background

A skinny straw is inserted into a solution of soap and water. When you exhale, gas
bubbles become trapped at the surface of the
water, forming a foam made out of very large
bubbles. A colloid has been created, and this is
a mechanical foam as well. Just think, you did
this as a little kid with your milk and now it's
actually a science experiment. This getting
older stuff isn't bad at all.

Next, after you clean your cup out, you
are going to add a small piece of dry ice to the
Toobe. The dry ice is going to produce bubbles
of carbon dioxide gas that you can see rising,
very rapidly, through the surface of the water and bursting. When you add
a squirt of soap to the water, the carbon dioxide will get trapped in the soapy
water, forming a foggy foam that grows and oozes out of the cup and down
the sides until it pops. Colloids, sublimation, and foam, oh my!

Setting the Trap ...

Ask for a volunteer and ask him to have a race with you to see
who can make the most bubbles in two minutes. Set two Toobes out
on the demo bench where the kids can see them. Each Toobe should
be full of water with a dash of soap and a straw sticking out of it.

Props

2	Toobes, or other container
1	1 oz. Bottle of liquid soap
	Water
2	9-inch Pie tins
2	Straws
1	Pair of tongs
1	Small piece of dry ice
1	Assistant
	Adult Supervision

The Zing!

1. Fill the Toobes, or other containers, three-fourths full with soapy water and put them in the pie tins to catch any spills. Demonstrate how to blow bubbles in the soap solution and imply that that is how the two of you are going to race. When your assistant is ready say, three, two, one, go!

2. Your volunteer should insert his straw down into the Toobe and start to blow bubbles in the solution. You will immediately notice that a herd of bubbles will start to rise up out of the container toward him. While he thinks he is off to a good start, it is now your turn.

3. Using the tongs, add a piece of dry ice to the water. *Dry ice* is very cold, 112 degrees below zero, and *should never be touched with bare skin*. Observe the bubbles of gas that are produced by the chunk of dry ice.

4. Because you added a couple of squirts of liquid soap to the water in the containers you will now have a major production of bubbles oozing up and out of the container. You win.

Things I've Screwed Up

Several small pieces of dry ice will produce more gas faster than one large piece of dry ice. The other important thing as far as showmanship goes is to keep the dry ice hidden in a coffee cup or some other place. Then there is more of an element of surprise.

The Instant Bubbler

How Come, Huh?

The first time around you were producing bubbles by blowing into a straw—a kind of mechanical foam. The air would leave your lungs, enter the liquid, and then be pushed to the surface.

In the second instance, the dry ice was sublimating—changing directly from a solid to a gas without taking time to become a liquid. The gas formed bubbles at the bottom of the tube, and being lighter than the surrounding liquid, they were pushed to the top of the Toobe.

Once the dry ice hits the top of the Toobe, the extremely cold carbon dioxide came in contact with the water-rich, room-temperature air and caused the water to immediately condense or form a mini-cloud. This cloud was trapped in the liquid by the soap bubbles and slid down the side of the container.

Take It & Run with It

19. Try this experiment without the soap and see how it affects the outcome. Explain why the soap is important.

20. Experiment with the recipe for the soap solution as well as the size of the straw, the opening on the straw, and other factors to create the longest, largest, string of bubbles.

Pushy Index Cards

A Little Background

A glass half full of water is covered with an ordinary index card. No adhesives of any kind are used to fix the card to the glass, it is simply sitting right on top of the rim of the glass.

The card and the glass are inverted, and the water remains inside the glass—another victory for air pressure. Now repeat the experiment, holding the card over the head of a volunteer.

Setting the Trap ...

Invite a friend to sit in a chair directly in front of you. Explain that you are going to do an experiment but, unfortunately, you are missing the lid to your glass. So, in the interest of science you are going to proceed, but the only thing you have for a lid is a piece of index card.

Look at the kid and apologize but explain that education must go forward. Please look directly up ...

Props

1   8-12 ounce Drinking glass
1   Index card, 4 inch by 6 inch
1   Unsuspecting assistant
     Water

INDEX CARD

WATER

CUP

Pushy Index Cards

The Zing!

1. Fill the glass three-fourths full of water. If you want to add an element of drama to this, ask your friend to examine the surface of the cup for adhesives, tape, sticky compounds, or anything else. Hopefully, she will not find anything on the surface of the rim.

2. Hold the glass and card directly over her head, and holding the card in place with your other hand, flip the glass upside down. Wiggle the card back and forth a couple of times—not much, just a little bit to set up a good seal.

3. Gently remove your hand from under the index card, and if everything goes well, the card and the water inside the glass will both stay in place. I have always wanted to have a heart-rate monitor on a kid when we get to this part of the experiment, just to see how much the heart rate changes.

If you are not successful, have your assistant towel off and try the experiment again with a new index card.

4. Assuming you are successful, you can now flip the glass back and forth several times with a quick twist of the wrist, and the card and the water will stay in place until the card warps to the point where it buckles and the water falls out.

Things I've Screwed Up

Be sure to wiggle the index card to get the seal with the first flip and don't try to flip the glass and the card too many times because it will buckle and soak your friend.

How Come, Huh?

We have about 100 miles of air pushing down on us at any given moment in time—one of the many blessings of living on a planet that has an atmosphere. All of this air creates about 14 to 15 pounds of pressure per square inch. This pushes on, over, and under everything on Earth. To bring this home put your hand on your forehead. For most kids this would be an area of 15 square inches. There is 225 pounds of air pressure pushing on your forehead alone—definitely a force to be reckoned with.

Back to the experiment. When you flipped the glass upside down, you were isolating the water and the bubble of air inside the glass. The combined weight of these two things is about 2 pounds. So you now have 2 *pounds* of pressure *pushing down* on the index card from inside the glass, but there is 15 *pounds* per square inch *pushing up* on the index card. When you think about approximately 100 pounds of air pressure pushing up against 2 pounds, it's not too hard to figure out who is going to win

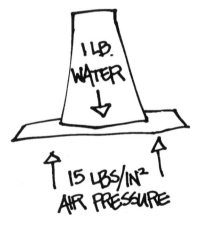

and why the card remains pushed up against the glass.

There are a couple of other factors that also help. By wiggling the card back and forth, you are creating a seal between the glass and the index card. This is due to the cohesion between water molecules—that is a whole different lab.

Bernoulli Toobe

A Little Background

You and your friend each have a very long, 9-foot, plastic Toobe that we call a Bernoulli Toobe—after Bernoulli's law—thank you for forgiving our spelling idiosyncracies. You challenge your bud to a tube-inflating contest. On your mark, get set, and you smoke the poor kid. Here's how …

Setting the Trap …

Unroll the large plastic Toobes that are about 8 feet in length that we call Bernoulli Toobes. Tell your friends that you would like to have a contest to see who can inflate the plastic tube the fastest. If you want to have fun, pretend like you have a chest cold, allergies, or chronic asthma while you challenge them to the contest.

To make the contest more interesting you will also offer to give said combatant a whopping 10-second head start on the inflation process. A recipe for sure defeat under normal circumstances …

Props

2   Bernoulli Toobes
2   Sets of lungs

The Zing!

1. At the appointed time say, "Go!" and watch your challenger start to huff and puff.

2. At the 10-second mark hold the opening of the Toobe up toward your mouth, but leave about six inches between you and the Toobe. Take a deep breath and blow as long and as hard as you can. What you will notice is that the Toobe will begin filling with air very rapidly. Your competitor is probably holding his Toobe directly over his mouth and filling at a much slower rate.

3. In a matter of seconds your tube will be full and your adversary will still be blowing into his. Youthfulness and treachery are once again victorious.

Things I've Screwed Up

Just practice, you'll be fine.

How Come, Huh?

This is a case of Bernoulli's law, of course. When you blow into the Toobe from a distance, you are lowering the air pressure at the mouth of the Toobe. This low air pressure is pushed into the Toobe by the higher pressure on the sides, filling the Toobe at a 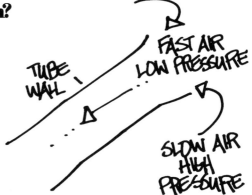 much faster rate than if you tried to fill the Toobe by blowing air from your lungs directly into the container. By leaving a space between your mouth and the tube, you are actually using the whole atmosphere to help you compete. Hardly fair.

Crushing Cans

A Little Background

You can tell your friends that you can crush aluminum cans without ever touching them. You'll just use the air in the room. This is done by taking an aluminum can and heating it in the flame of a propane torch. The hot can is then inverted in a pie tin half filled with ice water. The can is crushed, literally, by the air pressure in our atmosphere.

Setting the Trap ...

Place an aluminum can on the counter. Beer cans seem to work better than pop cans, but we will let you decide what is most appropriate for you. Tell your friends that you will be able to take the can and without even so much as raising a finger, crush the can completely.

The secret? They will ask. Stink eye. Every teacher uses it, every mom perfects it. Stink eye is the look you give a kid when he cuts into the lunch line, or generally behaves in a way that is deemed inappropriate by the powers that be.

Props

1   9-inch to 12-inch diameter pie tin
1   Cup of ice water
1   Pair of tongs
1   Aluminum can, 12-16 ounces
1   Propane torch
1   Book of matches
1   Pair of goggles
    Adult Supervision

The Zing!

1. Fill the pie tin half full of water and toss in a couple of ice cubes for good measure.

2. Place a clean, empty, aluminum can in the pair of tongs. Invert it so the opening is facing down and place it in the pie tin of ice water. Let the can sit there for about 30 seconds and observe what happens, if anything.

3. Nab the can in the tongs again, light the propane torch, and heat the can for about thirty seconds, rolling it around in the flame. When the can is nice and hot, invert it so the opening is facing down and place it in the pie tin of ice water.

4. What you will notice next is very entertaining. As the air inside the can cools, the air pressure outside the can will exert a force on that can and produce a shape that is very different from the one that you started with in the first place.

Things I've Screwed Up

Check the can for holes before you start. The best way to do this is to blow into the hole. You will be able to tell right away if there are any other holes. If so, find a different can.

How Come, Huh?

The first time you inverted the can the air pressure inside and outside the can was equal—there were no excessive forces placed on the can so there were no movement. The can retained its original shape.

Crushing Cans

When you heated the can, the air molecules inside the can started getting very excited and were bouncing around and off of each other. All this bouncing around caused the air inside the can to expand, and most of the air molecules were shoved out through the pop top opening of the can, which set the stage for the next part of the experiment.

When the can was flipped over a second time into the water, you created a closed system. No air could get in or out of the can. The air pressure outside the can pushing on the water was the same as before, but as the can cooled, the few remaining air molecules didn't take up very much space, which created low pressure inside the can.

This low pressure did not provide much resistance so the air outside collapsed the can as it pushed on it—much noisier than crushing the can against your forehead and more impressive too.

Take It & Run with It

21.   This experiment works very well with one-gallon metal cans with screw cap openings. Place a small amount of water inside the can, place the can on a stove. Heat the water until it is boiling then remove the can and cap it. Set the can on a level surface and allow it to cool. You will be very pleased with the results.

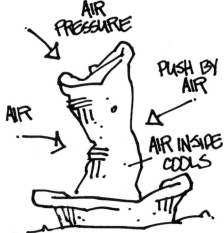

Funnel Frolics

A Little Background

You are going to learn two experiments that not only demonstrate Bernoulli's law, but also are a lot of fun to try on your friends. The first experiment requires that you tip your head back, place a funnel in your mouth, and place the Ping-Pong ball in the funnel. When you are ready, blow as hard as you can and try to get the Ping-Pong ball to pop out of the funnel. It won't happen.

Next bend over, point the funnel to the floor, hold the ball inside the funnel and start to blow. As long as you can blow hard, the ball will not drop to the floor. Neither result is "logical" or what you would expect from the natural world. That is, until you get to know it better.

Setting the Trap ...

Invite a friend to make a bet with you. If you have a twenty dollar bill to pony up, it makes it even better. Your friends will really sit up and take notice.

When you get your victim up in front, bet her that she can't blow a Ping-Pong ball out of a funnel, and that by blowing downward into a funnel you will be able to keep a ball from falling to the ground.

Props

2	Funnels
2	Ping-Pong balls
2	Set of lungs

Funnel Frolics

The Zing!

1. Ask your volunteer to tip her head back and place the funnel in her mouth. Then place the ball in the funnel, use the illustration to the right as a guide. Ask her to take a deep breath and blow as hard as she can to try to blow the ball out of the funnel to win the twenty bucks that you have riding on this experiment. It won't happen—we promise.

2. She will try and try and try to win that twenty, but the ball cannot be blown out of the funnel. It is against the laws of physics.

Next up, bend over with the funnel in your mouth. Hold the ball inside the funnel until you start to blow. Once the air is moving, let go of the ball and it will remain suspended inside the funnel until you run out of breath.

Things I've Screwed Up ...

Practice.

How Come, Huh?

Bernoulli's law states that the faster that air travels over the surface of an object, the less pressure it will put on that object. When you blow into the funnel, the air coming out is moving very fast compared to the air in the room. As this fast-moving air travels over the bottom surface of the Ping-Pong ball, it actually reduces the pressure on the side of the ball that is nearest to the opening. The other side of the ball remains unchanged, which means that you create a dramatic difference in pressure that always pushes the ball down into the funnel; and the harder you blow, the harder the ball is pushed into the funnel.

In idea #1 the ball is resting in the funnel. Gravity is holding it in place and you would think that a quick burst of air would pop it right out. However, when you blow into the funnel, you are reducing the pressure on the underside of the ball and actually forcing it farther into the funnel. Illustrations should help.

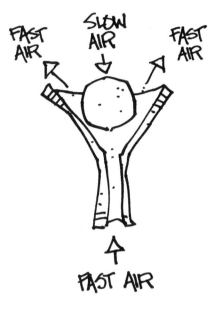

In idea #2 you are holding the ball in place until you can start blowing. Once the air starts traveling over the top surface of the ball, it reduces the pressure on that side, but the air pressure underneath the ball is great enough to hold it in place until you run out of breath—weird but true and definitely good for winning a couple of bets with your friends.

Take It & Run with It

22. Rig an air compressor up to a piece of PVC tubing and stick a funnel on the other end. Turn the compressor on, flip the funnel upside down and see if you can get the ball to be pushed up into the air stream. Bernoulli would be proud.

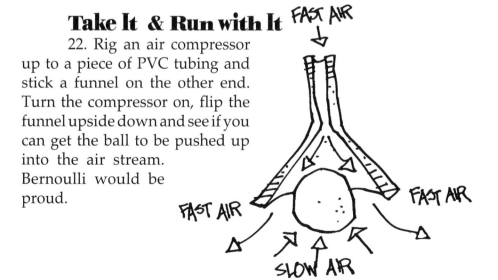

Ring of Fire

A Little Background

In this lab we are actually going to be able to see how a convection current moves by watching the behavior of an empty tea bag—that has been lit on fire and is burning.

The bag produces a column of hot air, and when the weight of the bag is reduced to the point where it allows it to be lifted up with the rising current of hot air, you have a floating, flammable tea bag.

Setting the Trap ...

Tell your friends that you have discovered how to levitate certain objects. Not all objects, just a few things like tea bags that are on fire. They, of course, will not believe you, but with a little practice you can make this very believable.

Props

1   Pair of goggles
1   Tea bag, paper
1   Pie tin
1   Book of matches
     Adult Supervision

The Zing!

1. Open the top of the tea bag and discard the contents of the bag. Pass the tea bag to your friend and ask her to examine the bag for wings, propellors, jet rockets, anything that might cause it to float, fly, or generally levitate.

2. Open the tea bag up so that it forms a cylinder and place it in the center of the pie tin. Remove any flammable items from the immediate vicinity.

3. Goggle up, and then light a match and touch it to the top of the tea bag in several places so that it begins to burn from the top down.

4. As the bag burns, feel free to invoke your magician's skills and "levitate" the bag.

Things I've Screwed Up

Not all tea bags are created equal. Be sure to test the tea bag before you do this demo in front of your friends.

How Come, Huh?

As the tea bag burned, the air directly above the bag was heated. Hot air rises, so it headed up and out leaving a vacancy. Cooler air replaced the hot air that rose toward the ceiling, and it too was heated by the burning tea bag—off to the ceiling and a convection current was created.

At a certain time in the experiment the mass of the tea bag had burned down to the point where it could be carried aloft by this current of hot air and so it lifted off the tin. Because it continued to burn as it floated, it perpetuated the convection current until all of the paper had been consumed.

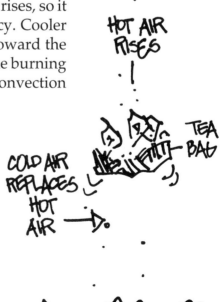

Memory Wire

A Little Background

Memory wire is the commercial name for a metal alloy made up of nickel and titanium called Nitinol. We tossed this in here because it is a metal that has unique properties. Instead of expanding when heated, it contracts, but even more interesting is that a particular shape can be set in a high-temperature furnace that the wire "remembers."

To demonstrate this property all you have to do is take the wire and bend it into loops, corners, and funny shapes, then hold it over a candle flame, and the wire contracts and "remembers" the original shape—which in this case is a straight wire.

Setting the Trap ...

Some inventions are so cool and so far out there that you don't really need to make up a story for them to be unbelievable. This is one of those labs.

Show your friends the wire. It is more or less straight. Bend it, wiggle it, make the outline of a duck—doesn't really matter—and then look at it like you screwed up. Make a face groan and mumble under your breath that you are going to have to start over.

Props

1   6-inch Piece of memory wire
1   Bowl with hot water or
    Hot water from the faucet
1   Candle, votive
1   Book of matches
1   6-volt Lantern battery
2   Alligator clips
    Adult Supervision

The Zing!

1. Turn the hot water on, and when it is as hot as it gets, slowly run the wire back and forth under the water. The heat from the water will straighten out the wire. Mutter something about "hard water" and bend the wire again.

If you do not have running hot water, then plunk the design in a bowl of hot water and watch it return to its original shape. Pull it out for the kids to see.

2. This will undoubtedly inspire some discussion. Make another shape and express your dissatisfaction again but this time apply heat in the form of a candle flame. Light the candle and move the wire back and forth under the flame. The heat will straighten out the wire real fast.

3. And for your grand finale, bend it one more time, express disgust a third time, and hook an alligator clip to each end of the wire, and connect it to a 6-volt battery. As the electricity flows through the wire, it generates heat. That heat will straighten out the wire, but it is a slower process

How Come, Huh?

Nitinol is an alloy of nickel and titanium, which bends quite easily at room temperature. When heated above a certain transition temperature—in this case 50°C, the crystalline nature of the metal undergoes a phase change, becomes hard, and assumes a previously set shape—in this case, straight. It is kind of like setting a mousetrap. You bend the wire and it sets the trap, the heat acts to release the metal from one form and the wire straightens out.

Ring & Ball

A Little Background

When solids are heated, they expand and get larger. When they cool, they contract. A set of brass rings and spheres—easily acquired through one of the science companies listed in the front of this book for about five bucks—are used to demonstrate this point. Once in your hands the set can be used to gather all the data necessary to demonstrate this principle using metals.

Setting the Trap ...

Tell your friends that you are confused about all of this expanding and contracting, heating and cooling of metals business—especially if you've just done the memory wire experiment for them. Write the information in the data table to the right on a chalkboard and ask your friends to go through and predict what will happen each time that you test one of the combinations.

Props

1   Set of ring and sphere
1   Propane torch
      or Bunsen burner
1   Propane torch stand
1   Ignitor or book of matches
1   Cup of ice water
1   Cup of room-temperature water

The Zing!

1. While they are both cool, insert the sphere in the ring and push it on through. This is Experiment #1 in the data table to the right. Record your results in the last column as *fit* or *did not fit*.

2. Continue with all of the different combinations listed in the table until the data table is complete. Analyze the data and write a general "law" describing how heat affects metal.

Data & Observations

Expt	Ring	Sphere	Result
1	Room Temp.	Room Temp.	
2	Hot	Room Temp.	
3	Hot	Ice Water	
4	Room Temp.	Hot	
5	Ice Water	Hot	
6	Hot	Hot	
7	Ice Water	Ice Water	

How Come, Huh?

At room temperature, the diameter of the sphere and the inside diameter of the ring are very close. When the sphere is heated, it becomes too large to pass through the ring. When the ring is heated, the sphere passes through easily.

Take It & Run with It

23. If you have not done the memory wire experiment, then you will want to throw it in reverse and have your friends try to explain that phenomenon, especially after you have done this lab.

Bimetallic Strip

A Little Background

A straight, thin, metal strip made of two metals pressed together—hence the name, bimetallic—is heated in the flame of a Bunsen burner or propane torch. As the bimetallic strip absorbs the heat from the flame, it begins to expand at different rates. This demonstrates the difference in the rates (or coefficients if you want to speak phybonics) of expansion for the two different metals.

Running the strip through a stream of cool water returns the strip to its original shape and also appears to have some element of magic to it. At least if you set it up that way.

Setting the Trap ...

Tell your friends that you have "polarized" water in the lab. It is a kind of water that will almost immediately straighten a bent metal rod and that you will demonstrate this phenomenon…

Props

1   Bimetallic strip
1   Propane torch
      or Bunsen burner
1   Ignitor
      or book of matches
    Source of running water
    Adult Supervision

The Zing!

1. Hold the bimetallic strip up and tell the kids that you have a special metal rod that, when heated in a flame, curves to the right. Place the strip in the flame and demonstrate this. As soon as the strip starts to heat, the metals expand at different rates causing a bow or curve to form.

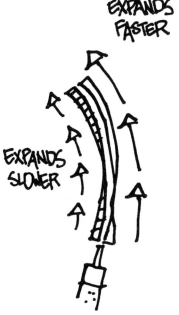

EXPANDS FASTER

EXPANDS SLOWER

2. Now to have some fun. Tell your friends that you have "polarized" water in the lab. It is a kind of water that will almost immediately straighten a bent metal rod.

Turn the faucet on and stick the very end of the now-curved bimetallic strip in the water and push it through slowly. As it hits the water, the metal cools, contracts back to its original position, and for the uneducated eye, appears to have been straightened out by the water.

How Come, Huh?

All metals expand when they are heated, but no metals expand at the same rate. With a bimetallic strip you have two dissimilar metals pressed together. When you expose them to heat, they begin to expand—each at their own rate. The metal that expands more quickly will push the slower expanding metal to one side. That is how the rod became curved.

When you placed the strip in water, the metals cooled and contracted. Just as metals expand at different rates, they contract at different rates. As the strip cools back down to room temperature, the metals in the strip contracted and the rod straightened out. Have fun with this one, it is good for several "ooh aahs" and quite a bit of noodle scratching.

Tazer Beams

A Little Background

If you wondering if we are now using non-lethal lab aids, you can rest assured that "tazer" is a contraction of talc and laser. It has nothing to do with stun guns or the like.

OK, so here's the concept. You cannot see light unless you look directly at the source, or the light waves reflect off a surface to your eye. You will demonstrate this by shooting a single beam of light across a dark room. You won't be able to see the light until you reveal it, using talcum powder.

Setting the Trap ...

Shoot a beam of light, either from the pocket lasers that are available for about five bucks or the flashlight that has been prepared according to the instructions below.

Have the kids look, but they will not be able to actually see the beam of light. That being the case, the logical question is, "Is it really there?"

CARD W/ HOLE

TAPE

FLASHLIGHT

Props

1   Index card
1   Hole punch
1   Flashlight
   or
1   Pocket laser
1   Roll of tape
1   Bottle of talcum powder
   or
1   Can of theatre fog
1   Dark room

The Zing!

1. Either buy a laser or using the hole punch make a hole in the center of the index card.

2. Tape the index card to the front of a flashlight so that the bulb is lined up directly with the hole in the card. Use the illustration to the left as a guide.

3. Darken the room and turn the flashlight on. Shine the light around the room and try to see the beam—not the dot of light reflecting off the wall, chair, desk, or other object, but the actual beam. You can't.

4. Holding the flashlight parallel to the ground or placing it on a tabletop to keep it steady, sprinkle a small amount of talcum powder where the beam of light appears to be shining. If your guess is correct, the beam will appear.

If you have a can of theatre fog, you can spray the fog in the room and take the flashlight—or a laser is even better—and wiggle it around so the kids can see the beam of light.

Things I've Screwed Up

There is a compound called titanium tetrachloride that is amazing. When it is exposed to air, it immediately reacts with the gases to produce huge volumes of white clouds. Great for this demo, but only if you were a Martian. One of the by-products of this reaction is dilute hydrochloric acid that rehydrates on the back of the throat of anyone in the room. Right, not a good idea.

Tazer Beams

How Come, Huh?

Light cannot be seen unless it is viewed directly at the source or is reflected off a surface to our eyes. In this case, the beam zipped through the darkened room undetected until it hit the wall or some other object and was reflected to your eye. When you sprinkled tal-

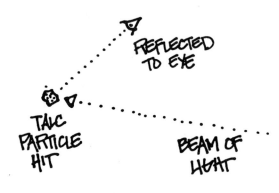

cum powder or sprayed the theatre fog, the air was filled full of little obstacles that reflected light to your eyes. As the zillions of particles of light traveled through the beam, many of them collided with the talcum powder/theatre fog and some were reflected to your eye.

Take It & Run with It

24. Arrange a series of mirrors so they are lined up to bounce light from one to another. Turn the lights off and the flashlight on. The beams of light traveling between the mirrors will be invisible until you walk around the room sprinkling talcum powder to reveal the light beams. This technique is used in a lot of spy and thief movies to reveal laser security beams crisscrossing the floors of museums and high-tech factories.

25. Figure out what other materials you can use to reveal a beam of light. Be sure to ask your mom before you start sprinkling baking soda and powdered sugar on the kitchen floor.

Visual Purple

A Little Background

The back of your eyeball gives residence to two different kinds of light-sensing receptors: rods and cones. The cones see color and the rods see black, white, and shades of gray. Our eyes adapt to darkness by producing a chemical called visual purple, which increases the ability of the rods to collect and transmit images in low-light situations. To increase the amount of light that enters the eyes, the diameter of the pupil (the black area in the middle of your iris) increases automatically. The increased amount of light and the production of visual purple makes it easier for us to see in darker places.

Setting the Trap ...

Tell your friends that light not only has the ability to illuminate things, but it also has the ability to cause your muscles to contract rapidly and decisively. They will automatically assume that you are talking about large, skeletal muscles, but that's OK—let them assume away.

Props

1   Dark room
1   Light switch
1   Pencil
1   Piece of paper

The Zing!

1. Ask your friends to pair up and stare into each others eyes. If there is one person left over, ask him to come be your partner.

Visual Purple

2. Darken the room and allow your eyes to acclimate to the dark for five minutes. Over the course of this experiment, as you read the text on this page, it should get noticeably easier each time you look at the page.

3. When your eyes have adjusted to the low light for a couple of minutes, draw a picture of your partner's eye on a sheet of paper and estimate the size of his pupil in millimeters.

4. Flip the lights on and observe what happens to the size of your partner's pupil as it is flooded with light.

5. Once the light is on, draw a second picture of what your partner's eye looks like, paying special attention to the pupil.

Things I've Screwed Up
Make sure that you give the eyes enough time to acclimate so that the pupils expand.

How Come, Huh?
As the light enters the eye, the brain recognizes that there is a tremendous amount of light flooding the cones and rods. It doesn't like this, so it closes the size of the opening to restrict the amount of light. If you go outside on a bright sunny day after being in a dark house, you may notice that there is so much light that it actually hurts your eyes, and you have to squint and look down at the ground for a minute until your eyes adjust.

"So, where do the muscles come in?" you ask The opening of the eye, the pupil, is regulated by ciliary muscles—thin, black, fibrous muscles that are driven by the involuntary reaction department in your brain. When the light floods the eye, the ciliary muscles contract and the pupil gets smaller. Light does make your muscles contract— or, at least, some of them.

Glass Rod Repair Shop

A Little Background

This lab is a fun zinger and a great way to introduce refraction and reflection. As it turns out, glass and some commercial types of corn oil have the same index of refraction. In other words, light bends at the same angle when it passes through either one. The interesting side bar is that it makes the glass objects inside the corn oil nearly invisible to the naked eye.

Setting the Trap ...

Announce that you have invented a new liquid that has the ability to restore broken glass to its original shape almost instantly. This is a claim that is quite hard to believe, so as you make the statement, add some credibility by taking the container with the oil and plopping it up on the table.

Props

1   Pint of Wesson corn oil
1   Roll of masking tape
1   Black pen
1   Drinking glass or 500-mL beaker
2   Glass rods
1   Hammer
1   Dishcloth
1   Glass eyedropper
1   Magnifying glass
1   Pair of goggles

The Zing!

1. Before your friends show up, fill a drinking glass or beaker with Wesson corn oil. Using a piece of masking tape, make a label that says, "Glass Rod Restorer."

Glass Rod Repair Shop

2. Place the label across the middle of the drinking glass. Place one of the two glass rods inside the glass with the corn oil. Make sure that it is completely submerged under the corn oil.

3. When your friends arrive, ask them to peer into the glass and look to see if there is anything there. You don't want to hand them the glass because they may catch a faint glimpse of the rod at the bottom, so simply hold the container at eye level and move quickly.

4. After the appropriate inspection period, hold a glass rod up and ask one of your friends to examine it. Upon confirmation of its entirety, goggle up, wrap the rod in the dishcloth, and smash it with the hammer. The smaller the pieces, the better. Be sure you wrap the glass rod thoroughly so none of the broken pieces fly out and hit anyone.

5. Empty the pieces into the drinking glass with the corn oil labeled "Glass Rod Restorer." Place the dishcloth over the beaker and inform your friends that it is now time to see just how fast this special solution repairs broken glass. Really.

6. After sufficient propaganda on your part, remove the cloth and reach into the jar to retrieve a whole glass rod to the astonished looks of your muchachos. Wipe the rod off and pass it around. If they ask you to repeat your performance, politely decline.

7. After the applause has died down, take a glass eyedropper and insert it halfway into the oil. It will appear to have a ghostly image, but will not be invisible until you squeeze the bulb and draw the oil up into the tube. When this happens, it appears as though the glass part of the eyedropper has disappeared.

8. And for your final experiment, gently dip a magnifying glass into the oil. You will notice that, unlike air or water, the light is not refracted and magnified.

Things I've Screwed Up

Check the glass and oil before you try the experiment. The refractive indices of glass, the purity of the glass, and the temperature as well as the quality of the oil all have an effect on the outcome of the experiment.

Indirect light also helps this experiment—things sometimes look better when the light is a bit dimmer. Ask any restaurant owner. If the light is reduced, the illusion is created more effectively.

How Come, Huh?

There are several parts to this explanation.

1. When light travels through the air and strikes the glass surface at an angle, a portion of the light is reflected. This is why we see the outline of the rod if it is placed in water or even waved around in the air.

Glass Rod Repair Shop

2. The rest of the light enters the glass rod, but as it does so, it is bent, or refracted, at an angle. The reason it does this is the light slows down when it goes from the air into the glass. In fact, all materials slow down light particles. This slowing is described as the index of refraction. The slower the light travels, the higher the index of refraction. Check out the first illustration.

Most materials bend light rays as they pass through them. The amount they bend the light is called the index of refraction and is measured as an angle.

3. In the case of the stirring rod and the Wesson oil, their indices of refraction are almost identical, which means that as the light passes through the oil and into the glass, it does not bend or refract enough to be detected by the human eye. See the second illustration.

If the index of refraction is equal for both objects, the light appears to pass straight through.

4. When you placed the glass eyedropper into the oil, it was full of air. The light entered the oil, zipped through the glass, and then hit the air. The index of refraction for the oil and the glass were the same, but the index of refraction for the air was different. So the light sped up and was bent, and as a consequence we could see the inside of the eyedropper. As soon as the oil entered the eyedropper, the index of refraction became uniform and the eyedropper was very hard to see.

Take It & Run with It

26. Try other glass items. Solid objects seem to work better than hollow items like test tubes or small beakers.

27. Rumor has it that heavy mineral oil also works well with glass. This can be acquired from your local pharmacy; it is sold as a laxative. If that does not work, try mixing heavy and light mineral oil.

28. Experiment with plastic containers and other liquids. See if you can find a liquid that refracts at the same angle.

29. Temperature also affects this experiment. Heat and cool the oil to different temperatures and observe the results. Create a model to explain why the temperature (density) of the oil would have an effect and use your studies to make predictions about other liquids.

UV Beads

A Little Background

This activity will make you look like the David Copperfield of light and color in the eyes of your friends. You are going to make the invisible visible. Ultraviolet waves are really out there. If you don't believe it, lie outside all day long some hot, sunny July day in your little bikini without sun block and then immerse yourself in a tub of hot water that same evening. What a wonderful sensation that is! You are feeling the effects of ultraviolet waves on your damaged skin cells. Not to mention the added benefit of looking like a lobster with a little white bathing suit painted on.

The first part of this activity is simply to observe a color change that occurs when the beads absorb ultraviolet light and then radiate visible light. The lab suggests testing the effects using sunblock.

Setting the Trap ...

Pass out the beads and ask your friends to tell you all the different colors that they see. They will probably only come up with white. Insist that there are at least five, maybe more, colors. They will disagree unless they are kindergartners and then they will see the colors with no problem at all.

Tell your friends that they need to go outside and paint the beads using sunlight. Be sure to check the expressions.

Props
5	Ultraviolet beads
1	Pipe cleaner
1	Egg carton
1	Piece of clear, plastic wrap
1	Roll of masking tape
1	Pair of scissors
1	Bottle of sunblock
1	Sun

The Zing!

1. String the five beads on the pipe cleaner.

2. Now, wear the pipe cleaner on your wrist, ankle, toe, or ear and quietly exit outside into the bright sunshine. Be sure to cover the beads so that the sun cannot reach them until you give the instructions for a group "ooh aah. "

3. On the count of three have your friends remove their hands and expose the beads to sunlight. Even on a cloudy day in the middle of winter in northern Minnesota you will get a color change—not as quick or as dramatic as in Phoenix in August.

4. Have your friends come back inside and notice that the beads change back to white in a minute or so.

5. Have your friends prepare their egg cartons by cutting a two-egg section from the bottom half of the tray. Have them take the beads off of the pipe cleaner and place two to three beads in each section of the egg carton. Put a piece of clear plastic wrap over one egg section and leave the other open.

6. Head outside once again and expose the beads to the sun. At this time, you may want to continue exploring the light-blocking abilities by using fabrics, colored paper, different strengths of sun block, or sunglass lenses

UV Beads

Things I've Screwed Up
You have to have a special gift to screw this lab up.

How Come, Huh?
Light is transmitted through electromagnetic waves, which means that they are measurable waves, usually 0.28 microns to 0.40 microns. The longer waves are generally attributed to causing the production of melanin and a nice tan; the shorter ones rip right through the cell and cream the nuclei. We call that cancer if it gets out of hand.

The ultraviolet beads used in this experiment contain a pigment that absorbs the ultraviolet light from the sun and then radiates it back to us as visible light.

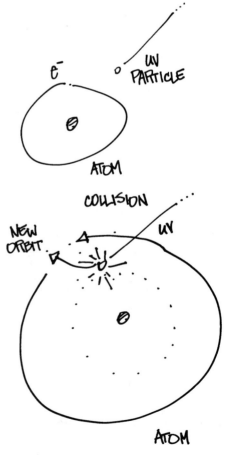

1. A photon of UV light zips away from the sun, travels 92,000,000 miles in about eight minutes, and zips through our atmosphere dodging numerous obstacles to smash into the pigment, which happens to be a molecule, embedded in the bead. You have just added energy to the molecule so something has to change.

2. The collision bumps one of the electrons (illustrated as e-) in the molecule from its regular, comfortable orbit to one that is a little bit farther away from the center of the atom. Translation: The energy from the light was absorbed by and stored in the electron's orbit, until ...

3.   This creates an unstable situation and the electron, wanting to get rid of this extra energy, emits it as light that we see and then returns to its regular orbit, where it continues to hover comfortably around the nucleus... until the next UV particle creams the electrons again which bumps an unsuspecting electron into a new orbit... and so it goes.

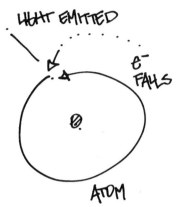

Take It & Run with It

30. Experiment with different sources of UV light. In addition to the sun try tanning beds, food-heating lamps, various lightbulbs, and UV lamps. Rate the amount of color change and determine how juiced each of these sources are.

31. Repeat the experiment using different brands of sunglasses. Check the glasses that are for sale in the store. Many of them claim that they block harmful UV rays. Place the UV beads in egg cartons and place the sunglass lens over each bead. Record the amount of the color change for each lens and rate them for their effectiveness.

32. Place the beads in the egg carton again and this time cover them with different materials such as black fabric, cellophane, wax paper, aluminum foil, and anything else you can think of to potentially block the UV rays. Record the color changes for each material.

33. The company that manufactures these beads also produces UV sensitive nail polish that changes colors in the sunlight. Design an experiment that uses UV sensitive nail polish.

Color-Mixing Discs

A Little Background

If you spin a black-and-white Holstein (cow) around and around in a farmer's field, will you begin to see a cow of many colors? No, but you might see stars if the cow regains balance and takes after you. Besides, cows are too big to spin. Let's use black-and-white patterns on a disc instead. In addition to spinning different patterns of black and white, you can also experiment with combinations of colors to get them to mix and produce secondary and tertiary colors as well. Crayons up!

Setting the Trap ...

Tell your friends that light not only has the ability to be split into the colors of the rainbow, but you can also take those same seven colors and mix them back together to make white light.

Props

3   Index cards, no lines
1   Empty quart can
     or other round object
1   Set of black-and-white patterns
1   Pair of scissors
1   Hole punch
1   Set of crayons or colored pencils
1   Drill, electric

CRAYON

PAPER DISK

The Zing!

1. Place the can on the index card and draw as many circles as you possibly can on each card; then cut them out. Make a hole in the very center of each disk using the hole punch.

TOP

2. Create the first four color combinations of discs listed on the data table below. Color half the disc one color and the other half the other color. Place the disc on the drill and give it a spin. Record the resulting color. If there are more than two starting colors, divide the disc equally.

Data & Observations

Disc	Colors	Resultant Color(s)
1	Blue/Red	
2	Blue/Yellow	
3	Red/Yellow	
4	Green/Yellow/Orange	
5		
6		
7		
8		

3. Once you have tried the first four combinations, then experiment with other color combinations of your own design. Be sure to fill in the data table above with your experiments and observations.

4. Using the pattern discs pictured on the next page, either copy or photocopy the patterns and put them on your drill (after you have removed the colored discs, of course). As you spin the discs, you will find that certain bands of color will appear at different locations on the disc or different illusions are created.

5. Spin each disc and record your observations in the data table on page 115. The blank discs (E and F) are for you to use to create combinations of colors or new patterns that you would like to explore.

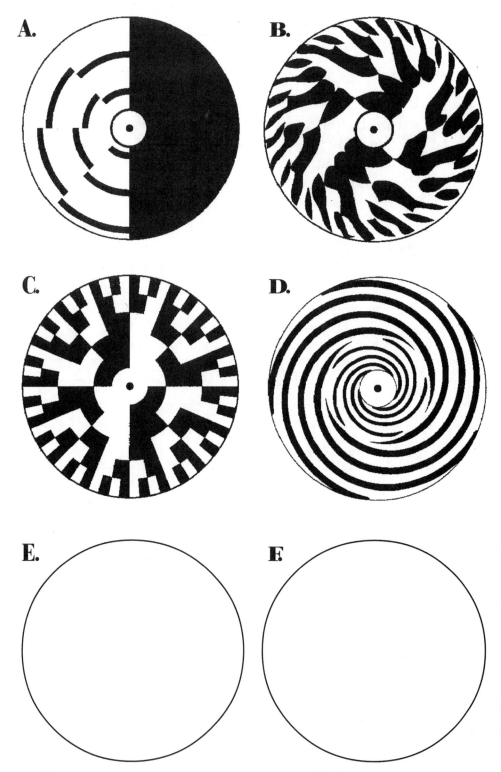

Color-Mixing Discs

Disc	Resultant Color(s) or Illusion
A	
B	
C	
D	
E	
F	

Things I've Screwed Up

This experiment works much better if you use a variable speed drill. Not everyone sees the same things at the same speeds.

How Come, Huh?

Why you see colors on the black-and-white-pattern discs is still somewhat of a mystery, but scientists believe it has to do with the cones that are located in the back of your eyeball.

There are three kinds of cones that collect each of the colors red, green, and blue. They also seem to process the information at different speeds. This is called the *latency time*. For example, red cones are the quickest to collect light information. They also dump the information to the brain the quickest. This is called the *persistence of response* time. Blue cones, on the other hand, are the slowest to collect and the slowest to send the information on. This helps to begin to explain why our brains think they see colors.

Color-Mixing Discs

As the disc spins, your eye sees alternating flashes of black and white. As the flashes of white light (made up of all the colors of the rainbow) hit your cones, the cones do not collect the colors at the same rate. Nor do they send that color information on to the brain at the same rate. It is kind of like the difference between eating buttered, salted popcorn by the handful versus eating a piece of popcorn, then salting your tongue, and then smearing a patty of butter across your tongue. You have the same basic components but much different perception by your brain.

This same response time is responsible for the mixing of colors when the color wheels spin. Your eyes will take the colors and send the information to your brain where it mixes the colors.

Take It & Run with It

34. The results you see are also affected by the direction in which the pattern is spinning. If you have a variable-speed drill, it probably also has a reverse. Try the pattern in the opposite direction.

35. The thickness of the lines also makes a big difference in the colors that you do or do not see. Experiment with the line thickness and the ability to see colors using the basic disc pattern A.

Ring Around the Rim

A Little Background

This experiment provides the opportunity for you to learn about sound vibrations and make an obnoxious irritating noise… all at the same time.

When you dampen your fingertip and rub it gently around the rim of a wine glass it will begin to emit a high-pitched sound. This continual ringing sound will soon begin to drive your cat into a frenzy sending it up the nearest tree. The exact mechanics of that will be covered in an entirely different book called *Catch a Wave*, which is a book all about sound.

Setting the Trap …

With young brothers and sisters you can tell them that if you tickle a wine glass by rubbing its rim you can make it sing. We are in the 3- to 5-year-old range here. With older friends a version of the truth is most amazing to them. Explain that by rubbing the rim you are pushing the air inside the glass back and forth (which is true) causing the glass to produce sound.

Props

3   Wineglasses, same size
1   Finger
    Water

The Zing!

1. Fill one wineglass a third full, a second two-thirds full, and the third glass almost completely full.

Ring Around the Rim

2. Dampen your forefinger and rub it gently around the rim of the first glass. As you rub, you will notice that the glass will begin to emit a faint hum. You are setting up a standing wave. Either slow down or speed up a little and the sound will get louder.

GLASS

AIR

3. Experiment with the different levels of water. Each glass will produce a different pitch, and when you get really good, you can tune an entire scale of wineglasses and play a song. The cat is already headed over the back fence.

Things I've Screwed Up

Every glass is different so you will want to practice. Speed is important only in that you want to set up a standing wave or a resonant wave and every glass is different in that aspect also. Faster is not necessarily better.

Aside from that the next most important thing is that the glass be clean. If oil from your fingers builds up on the rim, it becomes slippery. The reason this lab works is that the friction between your finger and the rim of the glass (the starting and stopping along the top edge) causes the glass to begin to vibrate. If you have lots of oil, the amount of friction will be reduced, and it will be more difficult to set up that standing wave.

How Come, Huh?

When you rub your finger around the edge of the glass, the glass begins to vibrate back and forth; this causes the air above the water in the glass to also vibrate back and forth. The less water there is in the glass, the longer the sound waves and the lower the pitch. By the same contrast, the more water in the glass, the higher the sound waves. The main thing that you want to take out of this lab for now is that sound is produced when an object vibrates.

Take It & Run with It

36. As you make the ringing sound with your glass, place a drop of food coloring in the water. Watch the results. You should be able to see the vibrations as the color mixes with the water.

37. Same idea as above, but this time add some sawdust or pencil shavings to the water. Watch the objects move on the surface of the water as the glass vibrates.

38. Create a neighborhood symphony. Nab a group of your friends and teach them how to make the wine glasses vibrate. Once they get the hang of it, fill the glasses with different levels of water and tune your orchestra.

39. Try different liquids in the glasses. Now you're messing with density. Try syrup, oil, Jello, glycerin, rubbing alcohol, etc.

Whooping Tubes

A Little Background

Acids and metals have never gotten along very well, and we are going to take advantage of that fact in this experiment. Dilute sulfuric acid is added to mossy zinc. When the two react, they produce a flammable gas and an odor that rivals any end-of-the-year gym locker. Not only that but this is a great demonstration of how expanding air produces sound.

Setting the Trap ...

Put your goofey face on and tell your friends that even test tubes have emotions. In fact, just like humans, test tubes holler when they are burned by a match. The proof is in the noise.

Props

1	Pair of goggles
1	20 mm by 150 mm test tube
1	Bottle of 2M sulfuric acid
3	Mossy zinc
1	Book of matches
	Water
	Adult Supervision

The Zing!

1. Once you've put your goggles on, add enough dilute sulfuric acid (2M) to the bottom of a test tube to fill it about 2 inches full. Drop a couple of pieces of mossy zinc into the acid and observe what happens. You should see small bubbles of gas forming and rising to the top of the tube.

2. After the reaction has proceeded for about 30 seconds, darken the room. Light a match and hold it near the mouth of the tube. You may want to apologize to the tube at this point in the presentation if you are really hamming it up. If you look carefully, you will see a bright blue flame ignite the gasses at the top of the tube and migrate to the liquid layer. When the flame gets to the liquid layer, the tube will produce a small "whoop." See... I told you the tube would complain.

3. This reaction will continue for several minutes. Be sure to let the tube have time to recharge (fill with gas). Relight the tube as many times as you can.

4. Turn the lights back on and gently waft the odor that is produced by the reaction. Never stick your nose directly over the tube and snort the gases into your nasal passages.

Things I've Screwed Up

Two things that mess this experiment up. One, be sure to get mossy zinc. It is manufactured using a process that incorporates iron into the finished product and speeds up the reaction. If your zinc is too "clean," you will not get the desired odor or reaction.

The other thing that can mess you up is having your sulfuric acid too dilute—2M is recommended for safety purposes, but if you are an adult, a dash of the straight stuff is always good.

SULFURIC ACID

MOSSY ZINC

TEST TUBE

Whooping Tubes

How Come, Huh?

The acid reacts with the zinc to produce hydrogen sulfide, rotten egg gas. This explains the smell. The hydrogen is flammable, so when the match is introduced into the mouth of the tube it ignites the gas. The whoop was caused by the rushing of hot gas out of the tube, which produced a vibration at the top of the tube when it escaped—the sound being produced by rapidly expanding air.

Take It & Run with It

40. Perform the experiments in tubes of different diameters and lengths. You will find that both the diameter of the tube and the distance between the top of the tube and the liquid level factor into the sound that is produced.

41. Any rapidly burning gas confined in a small space will produce a sound as it is escaping. With the permission of your parents research other flammable gasses and explore the possibilities for making noise.

Singing Rods

A Little Background

You will be able to create a vivid, not to mention quite annoying, demonstration of how compression waves can be amplified in a metal rod simply by stroking the rod with your fingers and a little pine pitch (rosin) to set up a standing wave—guaranteed to annoy all the dogs and most of the cats for a couple of miles.

Setting the Trap...

Sound sometimes gets trapped inside objects. True story. In this case the sound is trapped in a solid aluminum rod and the only way to get it out is to squeeze it gently, kind of like squeezing a tube of toothpaste. You pinch it in the middle and move it toward the end, and if you squeeze just right, sound will appear. Another incredible discovery of modern science!

Props

1   Set of fingers
1   Baggie of rosin
3   Aluminum rods
    Ear plugs (optional)

The Zing!

1. Dip your thumb and forefinger into the rosin and get a light dusting on them. Coat one-half of the rod with the rosin by rubbing your fingers back and forth on the rod.

It helps if you sprinkle some extra rosin on the top half of the rod and then spread it out with your fingers.

Singing Rods

2. Hold the rod right in the middle with your left hand, two fingers on top and thumb on the bottom. Take the thumb and forefinger of your right hand and "wipe" the rosin off the rod by moving your fingers down the rod, putting a fair amount of pressure on the rod while still moving at a pretty good clip.

Announce that you need to squeeze a little more. The trick is to set up the standing wave by squeezing or wiping the rod at just the right speed to amplify the sound—like everything else, it takes a little practice.

3. When you get to the end of the rod, you want to remove your fingers and quickly bring them back to the middle of the rod and rub again. At first it may take 15 to 20 seconds to get the rod to sing, but once you practice a while you can achieve an ear-splitting pitch in two or three wipes.

4. Here is the kicker, once you get the sound going, make a puzzled look. Announce that there is a second sound wave trapped in the rod and grab it one quarter of the way along the rod. This is an octave higher than the previous note.

Things I've Screwed Up

You want to give the rod a chance to resonate—which is why you want to lift your hand off the rod when you get to the end. It will take a little practice to get the octave above the first note. Just keep working at it and it will come.

How Come, Huh?

The rosin is sticky; it's pine pitch. The friction between your fingers and the rod caused the metal to produce a vibration, called a compression wave, that is travelling from end to end at very high speeds. Since the rod was cut to a resonant length, the waves almost immediately began bouncing from middle to end, multiplying the effect that you heard in the form of a standing wave.

Take It & Run with It

42. As you make the ringing sound with your rod, place one end of the vibrating rod in a bowl or bucket of water. Watch the results. You should be able to see the vibrations as the sound waves are transferred from the rod to the water.

43. Try using rods of different lengths to produce different sounds. When we demonstrate this lab activity, we use rods that are cut to 24 inches, 30 inches and 36 inches, which all produce dramatic results.

Kamikaze Straw Flute

A Little Background

You will need two naked straws for this experiment. Once in the buff, the straw is cut following the pattern on this page and flattened using a pair of scissors. Place the straw inside your mouth, just behind your lips, so that the ends are free to vibrate. When a large volume of air is pushed through the straw rapidly, it causes the cut plastic to vibrate, producing an obnoxious buzzing sound. Who needs fingernails on a chalkboard when you've got vibration?

Props

1 Straw, plastic
1 Pair of scissors
1 Pair of lungs

The Zing!

1. Flatten the end of the straw with a pair of scissors or your thumb. It may take several good hard rubs to get the straw flat.

2. Snip two small triangles from the end of the straw to produce the shape that you see to the right. It is important to make the cut steep enough to get a thin pair of "reeds" that will vibrate easily when you blow through the straw. The skinnier and taller, the better for producing sound.

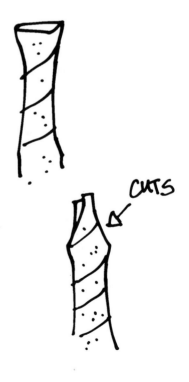

CUTS

3. Wet the cut end of the straw with your mouth, and with the straw inside your mouth and past your lips an inch or so, blow into the straw as hard as you can. The cut ends should vibrate and produce an obnoxious sound that resembles a duck with a bad head cold. If you have a difficult time doing this, it may be because you are not using enough air, or you need to put more of the straw in your mouth. Blow from your diaphragm (stomach area) and really push.

4. Once you have the straw flute down pat, take the scissors, and while you are blowing into the straw, cut the straw shorter and shorter, changing the pitch of the straw.

Things I've Screwed Up

The thing that hangs most folks up on this demo is not shoving the straw far enough into your mouth. The cut plastic has to have space to vibrate, so make sure the straw is at least an inch or so beyond your lips and is not resting against your tongue.

Another thing that happens is that when you cut the straw, sometimes the plastic ends stick together. Just pop them open with your fingers. And, finally, this requires a pretty good shot of air from your diaphragm. Give a good push of air from your belly and you should be easily mistaken for a duck during allergy season.

Kamikaze Straw Flute

How Come, Huh?

As the air passes over the opening that has been cut, it causes the cut ends of the straw to vibrate. The movement of the plastic compresses the air inside the tube, creating sound waves that come out the other end of the straw. The pitch of the instrument is directly proportional to the length. The longer the instrument, the lower the pitch and vice versa.

Take It & Run with It

44. Make straw flutes using straws of different diameters and different lengths to see if that has any effect on the pitch of the instrument that is produced. Or, take a second fatter straw and stick it over the end of the first straw and make a straw trombone. Who knows, maybe you can get a gig with Maynard Ferguson.

Alaskan Mosquito Call

A Little Background

The final lab in this section is a demonstration of the Doppler effect—sound vibrations. Plus every kid loves to whirl things over his head and make noise.

An artificial insect, which we are calling Doppler's Mosquito, is made using a paint stick, a rubber band, and a cork. The best part is that it actually buzzes like an insect.

Setting the Trap ...

Explain that everything in Alaska is bigger, including the bugs (rumor is that they can stand flat-footed and ring the doorbell ...). Just as with duck calls and moose calls, you can attract this giant mosquito with the right kind of instrument.

Props

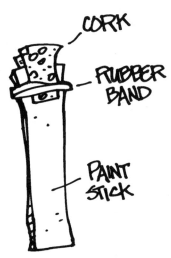

1   Cork
1   Knife
1   Paint stick
1   Hot glue gun
1   Glue stick
1   Rubber band, large, fat
1   Box of color markers
1   Spool of string
1   Pair of scissors
1   Pair of goggles

The Zing!

1. Cut a medium-size cork in half and notch the inside just a bit.

2. Place the paint stick in the notches and add a bit of hot glue to hold the two halves in place.

Alaskan Mosquito Call

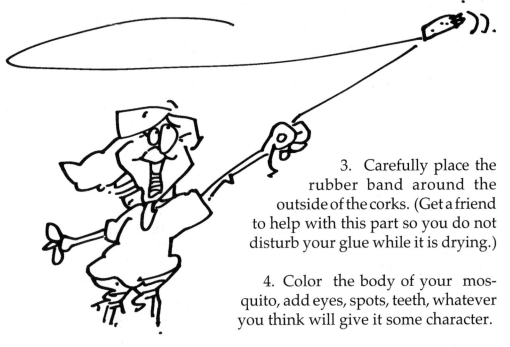

3. Carefully place the rubber band around the outside of the corks. (Get a friend to help with this part so you do not disturb your glue while it is drying.)

4. Color the body of your mosquito, add eyes, spots, teeth, whatever you think will give it some character.

5. Drill a hole in the other end of the paint stick and thread a 10-foot long piece of string through the hole.

6. Double it up and knot it so that you have a 5-foot-long piece of string hanging off the end of your mosquito.

7. Put on your goggles and get in an open space. Whirl the mosquito slowly around your head. Listen to the sound that you hear.

8. Now speed it up. Do you observe a different sound? Describe the two sounds. Do some research and explain how Doppler would describe the position and location of the sound waves as the mosquito whirled around your head.

9. Vary the length of the string and see if that has any effect on the sound waves and the pitch of the sound that is produced.

Things I've Screwed Up

Try not to hit anyone. There are two ways that you can effectively accomplish this: One, check the room before you start swinging and adjust for noggins; two, make sure that the string is tied tightly to the paint stick and won't fly off. Outside! Did we mention outside is a very good and safe place for this demo.

How Come, Huh?

The stick is deliberately constructed to be off center. As you spin it through the air it starts to spin. A flat stick produces a lot of vibrations in the air and can be heard from a long way away even if you are not a mosquito from Alaska.

Take It & Run with It

45. Make a bullroarer. You will need the following items.

1   Paper tube
1   Piece of elastic, 24 inches long
1   Spool of string
1   Pair of scissors

A. Thread the elastic through the paper tube and tie it off.

B. Cut a 10-foot piece of string. Double it up and tie it to the elastic.

C. Whirl the bullroarer over your head at different speeds and with different lengths of string. Listen to the sound that is produced and compare that with your mosquito.

Chain Reaction

A Little Background

We know that magnets exist. In fact, you probably have a fistful of them staring at you from the front of your refrigerator. So, this lab is designed to introduce you to the idea that the characteristics of a magnet can be induced, or passed, when certain materials simply come in contact with a magnetic field. In other words, that magnetism can be "passed" from one object to another and then to another with only the first object actually touching the magnet.

Your specific task for this lab is to take several different materials, and first of all, test them to see if they are attracted to the magnet. Then once you identify the materials that are attracted, you will test each item to see if you can hang a chain of those items from the magnet—proving the idea that the magnetic field in the magnet can be passed from one item to another.

Setting the Trap ...

This trap is best set for young kids, but I have caught older kids, just depends on how much science they have had. Speaking of which, did you know magnets can pass an atomic glue from item to item as long as they touch the magnet... it's true.

Props

1	Sheet of paper	1	Pair of scissors
1	Cow magnet	15	Small paper clips
15	Straight pins	15	Iron ball bearings (BBs)
15	Brass brads	5	Poker chips
3	Craft sticks		

The Zing!

1. The first thing that you are going to want to do is fill in the second column, Material, of the data table on page 134, by identifying what each material is made from. Your choices are metal, plastic, paper, or wood.

2. Cut several small pieces of paper from the sheet of paper. Each piece should be about half an inch wide and an inch long. You don't have to be exact. When the paper has been prepared, test each item in your data table with the magnet. Determine which ones are attracted to the magnet and which ones are not. Record your observations in the third column of the data table, Magnetic (Y / N), by writing a *Y* if it sticks to the magnet and a *N* if it does not.

3. You should have discovered in your testing that iron BBs are attracted to the magnet. Add an iron BB to the rounded end of the cow magnet. Then add a second iron BB to the first, then a third to the second, and so on. Use the illustration below as a guide.

4. Hang one BB off the end of the previous one. When you can no longer add any BBs to the chain, record the *maximum* number of iron BBs that are hanging off the cow magnet. This number can be entered next to BBs in the fourth column named, # *Items Hung*.

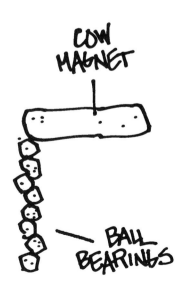

5. Repeat this procedure with the other objects that were attracted to the magnet. Record the *maximum* number of each item you test in the data table.

Record the *maximum* number of items that you got to hang off of the cow magnet in the data table on the next page.

Chain Reaction

Item Tested	Material	Magnetic (Y/N)	# Items Hung
Straight Pins			
Poker Chips			
Paper Clips			
Brads			
Craft Sticks			
Ball Bearings (BBs)			
Paper Strips			

How Come, Huh?

The iron particles in the magnet are organized and lined up in an orderly fashion. When this happens, a magnetic field is produced that attracts other iron objects. When these other iron objects come close to the magnet, they also line up in the magnetic field of the magnet, and this produces another, weaker magnetic field. At some point the weight of the object is greater than the magnetic field that is attracting it, and it falls off the chain. The brads don't work at all because they are made of copper and steel and do not have enough iron to be attracted to the magnet. Paper is not magnetic and neither is plastic or wood, but we'll let you prove that to yourself in another lab, at another time.

Take It & Run with It

46. Re-create the experiment and use the same materials, but substitute different kinds of magnets. Create a data table that allows you to record the strengths of the different magnets that you test and then graph that data for easy comparison.

47. Design an experiment that explores how the shape of a material affects its ability to form chains. For example, BBs, straight pins, and paper clips are made of iron that has been formed into different shapes. Find three other iron objects that also have different shapes and determine if the shape of an object affects its ability to form chains.

48. Do this experiment with a friend so she understands the idea you are exploring and then write sequences of different objects on a piece of paper and ask her to predict if and where the chain will fall apart. For example; Chain 1: paper clip, paper clip, BB, brad, pin, BB, and pin. Chain 2: BB, BB, pin, paper clip, BB, pin, and brad. Chain 3: brad, brad, BB, pin, paper clip, and pin. Take turns inventing chains and testing each other.

49. Make a chain of BBs hanging off the end of a magnet. Gently remove the chain from the magnet by grabbing the top BB. Hold the chain of BBs over the palm of your hand and watch as the BBs fall off one by one. Why did they fall off?

Pinching Water

A Little Background

By now you should know that water molecules are very friendly with one another. They are great buddies and love to hang out together. In this experiment you are going to take two streams of water that are diverging, or going separate directions, and with a pinch of a couple of fingers, they will converge, or come together—until you flick them and they separate back into two streams.

"And just why does this happen?" you ask. Water molecules act like minature magnets with a positive and negative end.

Setting the Trap ...

Ask your friend to hold a soup can full of water that has a piece of tape covering two holes. Position the can so that when you remove the tape, the water falls into a tub. Tell your buddy that you are going to remove the tape and two streams of water will begin falling out of the can. His job, before all the water falls out of the can, is to glue the two streams of water together.

Ready? And here we go… panic sets in immediately.

Props

1   #303 Soup can
1   Hammer
1   Nail, 16-penny
1   Roll of tape
1   Tub or sink
     Water

The Zing!

1. Prepare two small holes near the bottom of the soup can. The holes are best placed one-half inch from the bottom seam and one-half inch from each other. Use the illustration to the left as a guide.

2. Place a small piece of tape over the holes and fill the can with water.

3. Hold the can over the sink or tub and remove the tape from the holes. The water should start to empty out of the can through the two holes. You will notice that the two streams of water diverge, or separate and go different directions. Take your thumb and forefinger and literally pinch the two streams of water together. When you remove your fingers, the streams should be one.

4. The water should continue to flow as a single stream. To separate the streams of water simply give them a flick. Once they are separated, they stay separated.

Things I've Screwed Up

One half an inch seems to be the perfect distance between holes. Closer than that and the streams have a tendency to come together spontaneously, which ruins the effect, and more distance between the holes and the streams of water tend to separate spontaneously, which also shoots your presentation in the foot. Build it and practice.

Pinching Water

How Come, Huh?

If you could see a water molecule, it would look like the outline of Mickey Mouse's head. A big, fat oyxgen molcule in the center with two smaller hydrogen atoms stuck up on the sides that look like ears. This arrangement of atoms makes the atom behave like a little magnet. The hydrogen atoms are positively charged, and the oxygen atom has a negative charge.

When polar water molecules from the two streams come in contact with one another, they adhere, or stick, to one another forming a single stream. By pinching the water you are simply moving the streams of water molecules close enough together for them to be attracted to one another and form a single stream.

When you flick the single stream of water, you are literally separating the two streams, and they are just far enough apart that they cannot attract and hold one another.

Take It & Run with It

50. It works with two streams, how about three? Four?

51. Determine the "tolerances" for hole placement. In other words, how far apart is too far and how close together is too close?

52. What happens if you place the holes on top of one another and the streams of water are lined up vertically instead of horizontally? Can you still pinch them together?

Flying Paper Clips

A Little Background

Another challenge for you to ponder. Make a paper clip float in the middle of the air. If you solve this problem, you will create an illusion of a paper clip flying away from the ground, restrained only by a thin thread. Be sure to have your magnetic fields ready to go.

Setting the Trap ...

Pass out paper clips, a piece of tape, and thread to your pals. When they have their materials, inform them that their task is to take all three components and create a situation that allows the paper clip to hover in place, in midair.

Props

1	Length of thread, 2 feet or so
1	Paper clip, small
1	Chair
1	Piece of masking tape, 2 inches
1	Pair of scissors
1	Cow magnet
1	Table
1	Metric ruler
1	Bar magnet

The Zing!

1. Tie one end of the thread to the paper clip. Tape the other end of the thread to the seat of the chair.

Flying Paper Clips

2. Balance the cow magnet so that one end sticks over the edge of the table.

3. Hold the paper clip up and slide the chair toward the cow magnet until the magnetic field of the cow magnet is strong enough to attract the paper clip.

4. Release the paper clip and it will appear to levitate in midair. If you don't get it right away, change the angle that the paper clip flies, making it steeper. Or, you can try getting the paper clip very close but not touching the magnet. Play with the idea and have fun.

5. When you get the paper clip to fly, fill in the data table. Then repeat the experiment using a bar magnet (or magnet of your choice) and fill out the data table.

Things I've Screwed Up

The stronger the magnet, the better. Cow magnets are very strong as are the neodium kind. If you have a small or weak magnet, you will have a more difficult time getting the paper clip to hover.

Another trick that helps is to increase the angle that the paper clip hovers relative to the chair. The steeper the angle, the easier it is to get it to stay in place.

Data & Observations

When you get the paper clip to fly, record the exact measurements that you used to get this experiment to work.

Length of string _____ cm
Distance of paper clip from *cow* magnet _____ cm

Length of string _____ cm
Distance of paper clip from *bar* magnet _____ cm

How Come, Huh?

The magnetic field of the magnet extends well beyond the physical border of the iron. This magnetic field reaches out and attracts the iron particles in the paper clip. The attraction is strong enough to overcome the force of gravity, and the mass of the paper clip being pulled toward the Earth, so it appears that the paper clip is flying.

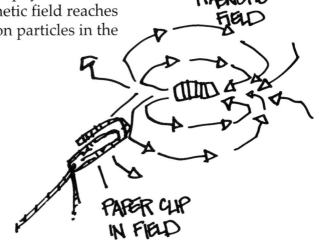

MAGNETIC FIELD

PAPER CLIP IN FIELD

Take It & Run with It

53. Add paper clips to the experiment. See if you can get two, three, four, or more paper clips on their own individual strings, flying toward the same magnet.

54. Fill a small baggie with iron filings and see if you can re-create this experiment.

Overhead Mag Fields

A Little Background

You can "see" the magnetic field that surrounds a magnet using iron filings, an overhead projector, and a strong magnet.

According to the musings of many scientists you cannot only detect but also "see" the magnetic field that surrounds magnets using iron filings. They contend that the reason this is possible is because the iron filings will align with the lines of forces radiating out from  the poles of the magnet when it is placed next to or near the iron filings. By sprinkling the iron filings around the magnet and recording the position of the particles you will be able to infer, or figure out, the direction of the magnetic field surrounding any magnet.

Setting the Trap ...

Tell your friends that all magnets have invisible magnetic fields, which is true. And, in order to see these magnetic fields and at the same time spice up your lab, you are going to sprinkle pepper over and near the magnet to reveal the magnetic field.

Props
1 Cow magnet
1 Sheet of plastic for overhead projector
1 Bottle of iron filings in pepper shaker

The Zing!

1. Put the cow magnet in the middle, under the plastic sheet.

2. Sprinkle the iron filings all over the top of the sheet of plastic. When you are done, tap the edge of the plastic so that the filings will align with the magnetic field of the magnet and reveal the pattern more clearly.

3. Have your friends describe what they see and how it is possible that iron filings would be attracted to a magnet.

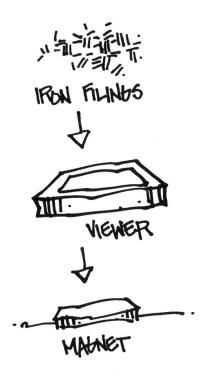

IRON FILINGS

VIEWER

MAGNET

How Come, Huh?

The iron filings are influenced by the lines of force radiating from the magnet. As the lines of force bend, the filings will align to reflect this force. By mapping the position of the filings at various spots around the magnet, you are plotting data points. By connecting the filing lines, you will get a rough picture of what the magnetic field looks like.

Take It & Run with It

55. Get a larger chunk of paper and see how far out you have to go before the magnetic field becomes undetectable and the Earth's magnetic field takes over. Try it with different magnets.

3-D Magnetic Fields

A Little Background

Most of the time folks see magnetic fields as flat, two-dimensional configurations when in actuality they are three-dimensional. The problem is that the way we look at magnets most of the time does not allow us to see all three dimensions. We are going to change that with this lab.

We are going to incorporate a very strong magnet used by cattle ranchers called a cow magnet. It is inserted into the first stomach of range cattle. That way when these silly animals eat barbed wire and old tin cans, the metal stays in the first stomach and does not pass through the system causing bleeding.

Setting the Trap ...

No trap, just tell your audience that you are going to produce a three-dimensional magnetic field using a cow magnet and big pile of iron filings.

Props

1   Bottle of iron filings
1   Clear, clean, 16-oz. bottle
1   Cow magnet
1   Plastic test tube
1   Bicycle-tube section, 3 inches
1   Rubber band

The Zing!

1. Pop the lid on the iron-filing shaker and empty about half the bottle into the pop bottle that you have previously checked to make sure it is clean and dry.

2. Slide the cow magnet into the plastic test tube. Make sure that it slides all the way to the end.

3. Place one end of the bicycle-tube section over the plastic test tube. Slide the tube inside the bottle and fold the other end of the bicycle tube over the mouth of the bottle.

This will enclose the bottle and keep the iron filings from flying all over the place. Use the illustration to the right as a guide.

4. When you are ready, give the bottle a couple of good shakes. This will toss the iron filings up into the air, and they will come in contact with the magnetic field of the cow magnet. As the iron filings stick to the test tube, a three-dimensional picture of the magnetic field will appear. Pay special attention to the concentration of filings near the poles as well as to the orientation of the iron filings near the middle. This clearly demonstrates that the strength of the magnet is in the poles.

5. When it is time to clean up, simply lift the magnet gently up toward the mouth of the bottle and roll the bicycle-tube section back. When the magnet is completely out of the bicycle-tube section, the iron filings will fall back into the bottle.

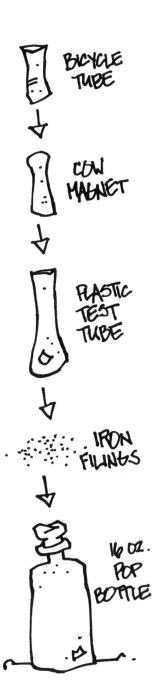

BICYCLE TUBE

COW MAGNET

PLASTIC TEST TUBE

IRON FILINGS

16 OZ. POP BOTTLE

3-D Magnetic Fields

Things I've Screwed Up

Use a plastic test tube, they are less expensive and much harder to break when you slide the cow magnet in and out of the tube. You can get old bicycle tubes from a bike shop. They are more than happy to wave as you walk out the door with their garbage. Degreased iron filings tend to be less messy. Those are the big three: plastic tubes, free tire tubes, and cleaner iron filings. Nature will take care of the rest.

How Come, Huh?

The cow magnet has a very strong magnetic field. As the iron filings are tossed around the inside of the bottle, they are attracted to the magnetic field that radiates out from the magnet. Because the filings are small and can be influenced to move in any direction, they align with the lines of force and create a three-dimensional picture of the magnetic field.

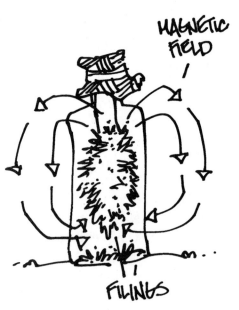

When you slide the cow magnet out of the test tube, the magnetic field goes with it and the iron filings fall back to the bottom of the bottle because they are no longer being pulled into orbit by the cow magnet.

Take It & Run with It

56. We can't think of any good extensions but thanks for reading this far anyway. Lab up!

Eddy Currents

A Little Background

An eddy current is created when a strong magnet drops through a metallic (but not iron) tube. The effect, as you will see, is much different than if you were to drop a nonmagnetic object through the same tube.

Setting the Trap ...

Tell your friend that she is going to participate in the experiment today as a timekeeper.

Show your friend the cow magnet and ask her to examine the two tubes that you have. She is to inspect the tubes to make sure that they do not have any residue, barbs, screens, or other obstructions. When it has been confirmed that they are free and clear of anything, ask your friend to time how long it takes a magnet to fall through each of the two tubes that you have. Once you have the times collected, reinspect the tubes and try to figure out why you got the data that you did.

Props

1   PVC pipe, 1 inch diam., 3 feet long
1   Wooden dowel, 0.75 inches by 3 inches
1   Cow magnet
1   Metal pipe, 1 inch diam., 3 feet long
1   Watch with sweep-second hand
1   Assistant

Eddy Currents

The Zing!

1. Hold the PVC pipe straight up and down, like the illustration to the right, and drop the wooden dowel through the tube. Ask your assistant to record the amount of time that it takes for the dowel to travel the full length of the tube. Enter that number in the *Data & Observations* section below. Repeat the test three more times and then determine the average speed.

2. Repeat the experiment using the cow magnet. Record these times in the data table.

3. Repeat the experiments again, this time using a metal, but not iron, tube. Drop the cow magnet and the wood dowel through each tube three times and average the data you collect.

Data & Observations

Tube	PVC			Metal		
Object / Trial	1	2	3	4	5	6
Dowel						
Cow Magnet						

Things I've Screwed Up

The closer the diameter of the tube is to the outside diameter of the cow magnet/wood dowel the better this experiment works. If the tube is either too narrow or too wide, you will find that the data will not produce the aberration that you are looking forward to seeing.

How Come, Huh?

When you drop the magnet into the metal tube, the magnetic field surrounding it constantly changes as it falls. This changing field induces, or starts, the flow of eddy currents in an electrical conductor. These eddy currents produce a magnetic field that repels, or pushes, against the falling magnet, causing it to slow down.

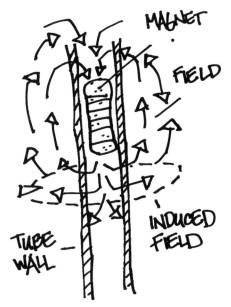

Take It & Run with It

57. Experiment with different kinds of metal tubes. See if you can rank the different kinds of metals in order of their ability to produce eddy currents and resist the movement of the magnets.

58. Try magnets of differing strengths and see if this affects the size and strength of the eddy currents that are produced. The stronger the currents, the slower the magnets will fall.

59. Determine if the length of the tube has any effect on the speed the magnet falls or the amount of time that it takes for the magnet to emerge from the pipe's end.

A Simple Motor

A Little Background

Everything that you have been studying—all of the ideas that you have been poking and prodding—lead to your understanding of this one, big, idea: how a simple electric motor works. So, nab your eddy currents, flying paper clips, friendly water molecules, and magnetic fields so we can wrap them into a new project.

We are going to use permanent magnets to create the magnetic field, a coil of wire to form the actual motor, and a felt marker will stand in for a decent commutator. Once you build this version, we will turn you loose on the world and let you figure out more sophisticated models—but first things first.

Setting the Trap ...

Pass out the materials: cup, magnet, paper clips, and coil of wire. Tell your friends that you want them to make a working motor from the parts that you have given them. Depending on their backgrounds you will find all kinds of solutions to your problem.

Props

1   D Battery
1   D Battery holder
2   Alligator leads
4   Donut magnets
1   12-oz. Plastic cup
1   Roll of masking tape
2   Paper clips, large
1   2-foot Length of bell wire
1   Pair of wire strippers
1   Black, felt marker, permanent

The Zing!

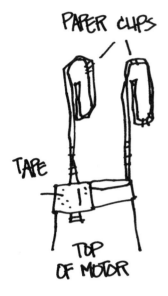

PAPER CLIPS

TAPE

TOP
OF MOTOR

1. Insert the battery into the battery holder and attach one alligator lead to each terminal.

2. Make a stack out of the four donut magnets. Divide the stack in half and place two magnets inside the bottom of the cup and two additional magnets outside the bottom of the cup.

3. Open the paper clips up and tape the extended portion of the paper clip to the bottom of the cup on either side of the magnets. Use the illustration to the left as a guide.

4. Leave a 2-inch tail and start to wrap a coil around two fingers on your hand. Wrap until all of the wire is used up, leaving another 2-inch tail.

Use the tails to make a single wrap around the coil and hold it in place. Adjust the tails so that they are sticking straight out. Strip two-thirds of the plastic off each tail.

5. Using a permanent marker, blacken the top half of each tail. Be sure to blacken the same side on both tails.

A Simple Motor

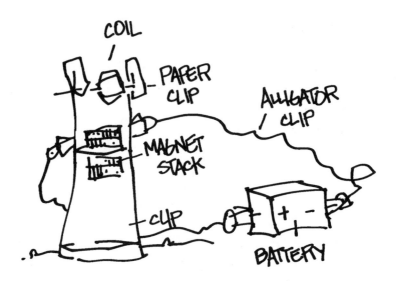

6. Slide the coil of wire into the supports. Use the illustration above to help you.

7. Clip one alligator lead from the battery to the base of each paper clip. When you connect the second lead, you will notice that the coil did one of three things, 1) started spinning, in which case you do nothing but holler, "Yahoo!" and shove your fist in the air, 2) wobbled, in which case give the coil a gentle twirl and it should start to spin, or 3) did nothing and you are going to have to troubleshoot. See below, please.

Things I've Screwed Up

If your motor does not spin, try these things in this order.

1. Check your battery and make sure that it has juice.

2. Make sure that the alligator clips are connected to the metal tabs in the battery holder and not to a piece of the plastic.

3. Double-check the connection between the clip and the insulated wire; check for breaks in the alligator wire.

4. Straighten the tails coming from the coil. The coil should spin smoothly and without much wobbling when you spin it with your finger. If it does not, flatten the coil a bit and straighten the wire.

5. Check the position of the paper clips. They should be even. If one is higher than the other, the coil will be lopsided and have to work harder to spin. Make sure they are level.

6. Add a second battery for more juice or substitute either a lantern battery, a 6-volt, or a variable, low-volt, power supply. By now your motor should be spinning. We have built thousands of these things and one of the reasons that we selected this design is because it is so kid- and adult-friendly—virtually any electrical nincompoop can build one.

After your motor spins for a while, you may notice that it starts working less efficiently. This is usually because the marker gets a little smeared. Clean the wire with a paper towel and re-mark the wire. Another common problem is that kids build these things, run them for hours, then they start to fritz. They readjust everything and still no spin. Get a new, fresh battery and this will solve your problem 99 percent of the time.

How Come, Huh?

The four magnets formed a permanent magnetic field. When you hooked the coil of wire to the battery, a magnetic field was produced around the coil. When these two magnetic fields come into close contact, there is movement. The coil starts to move, but only temporarily.

It is temporary because you blackened the top half of each tail.

A Simple Motor

This black ink served as an insulator so that when the coil makes half a spin, the electricity stops, the magnetic field disappears, but the coil continues to spin because it has momentum. When it completes its cycle, it comes in contact with the bare wire again, juice flows, magnetic fields are created, and the coil gets another push. Think of a bike that has been flipped upside down. You whack the wheel and it spins, you whack it again and it spins faster, you keep whacking the wheel each time it comes around and you have a lot of motion—same idea here.

Take It & Run with It

60. Prove that the amount of electricity is directly proportional to the speed that the motor will spin.

61. Figure out other ways to insulate the top half of the wires that form the coil supports. Or, read up on commutators and figure out how to add one to your motor.

62. Experiment without insulating the coil supports.

The Neutron 'Do

A Little Background

According to our current understanding of science, static electricity can be generated by rubbing two objects together. You are going to prove that idea using a rubber balloon to steal a couple of billion electrons from a pile of very fine hair and in the process create some very interesting and very funny special effects.

For the record, static electricity experiments work best when the humidity is low—or at the very least when it is not raining. If you live anywhere east of the Rocky Mountains and are reading this during the summer months, we would highly recommend skipping to another portion of the book. Just a thought.

Setting the Trap ...

Invite a friend to help with the demo and ask her if she brought her electrons with her. She will usually give you a silly-to-confused look and either not know what you are talking about or simply tell you that she did not bring the electrons with her today.

At this point you assure her that she did bring her electrons and that you would like her permission to collect a few billion of them so that you can conduct a science experiment.

Props
1   Balloon, 9 inches, round
1   Pile of hair, fine
    Low humidity, preferably

The Neutron 'Do

The Zing!

1. Inflate the balloon and tie it off. Hold the inflated balloon next to the hair on your volunteer's head. Wave the balloon around a bit and see if you can get the hair to stick to the balloon.

2. No luck, huh? Take the balloon and rub it back and forth vigorously on the head of the person with the fine hair. After 15 to 20 rubs, gently lift the balloon off the top of her head keeping contact with the hair strands. Observe what happens when you move the balloon back and forth over your volunteer's head.

3. Now remove the balloon completely and take a peek at what happens to the hair. Bring the balloon back, near the volunteer's head again and observe the hair strands. Remove the balloon again.

4. We have pretty much established the fact that hair releases electrons to a rubber balloon, which carries the charge. The lingering questions is, "Does all hair provide the same amount of electrons?"

Data & Observations

Write the name of the person that you are testing in the first box. Hair color can be abbreviated as: Blonde: Bl, Black: Bk, Brown: Bn, Red: R, and White/Gray: W. Type can be abbreviated as: Coarse: C, Medium: M, Fine: F., and length can be abbreviated as: Short: S, Medium: M (shoulder-length), and Long (beyond shoulders).

I predict that _____ (length), _____ (color), hair of a _____ texture will produce the most electrons when it is rubbed with a balloon.

Name	Hair Color	Type	Length
1. _____	_____	____	____
2. _____	_____	____	____
3. _____	_____	____	____
4. _____	_____	____	____
5. _____	_____	____	____
6. _____	_____	____	____
7. _____	_____	____	____
8. _____	_____	____	____
9. _____	_____	____	____
10. _____	_____	____	____

The Neutron 'Do

How Come, Huh?

When we start out, every-thing is balanced. The balloon has the same number of electrons and protons and the charge on the hair shafts is balanced. In a balanced atom there is one electron for every proton and vice versa.

When you rub the balloon on the head of the person with the fine hair, the rubber in the balloon attracts the electrons from the hair—rubber does that. This does two things. One, it steals negatively charged electrons from the hair shafts. This leaves the hair with a net positive charge; and two, steal-ing electrons increases the negative charge on the balloon. If you have hair with a positive charge and a balloon with a negative charge, that goes a long way to explain why the hair is attracted to the balloon.

What you should have found by testing different kinds of hair is that fine hair works the best. Color and length tend to not have any effect on the ability of the hair to donate electrons. The one determin-ing factor is the thickness of the hair. The reason for this is that finer hair has a greater surface area. A greater surface area means that more electrons are exposed to the rubber surface of the balloon.

Take It & Run with It

63. Once you have experimented on human hair, why not branch out to other animals? Nab the neighbor's cat and see if a charge can be generated there. Try your dog, rabbit, gerbil, or pet llama.

Wiggly Water Streams

A Little Background

If you could see water molecules, they would look like Mickey Mouse's head: a big round oxygen atom in the center and two little hydrogen atoms tucked up on top. The illustration to the right should give you the general idea.

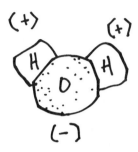

This kind of configuration is called a bipolar molecule. The reason chemists call it that is because hydrogen atoms have a positive charge and oxygen atoms are negative. Positive on one end and negative on the other, and you have a molecule that behaves like a little magnet. Since there are two poles, they call it a bipolar molecule, which makes perfect sense to us.

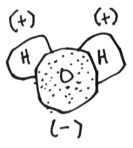

Setting the Trap ...

Announce that you have been working on a new idea and for the entertainment of the family you have taught the water faucet to dance. Well, not the water faucet itself but the water coming out of the faucet.

Props

1   Balloon, 9 inches, round
1   Pile of hair, fine
1   Faucet with running water
    Sink

Wiggly Water Streams

The Zing!

1. Inflate a rubber balloon and tie it off. Rub it back and forth vigorously on the head of a person with fine hair. This will build up a huge negative charge.

2. Turn the faucet on and get a very thin, continuous stream of water dribbling out of the faucet. Bring the charged balloon near the water, which will be attracted to the balloon.

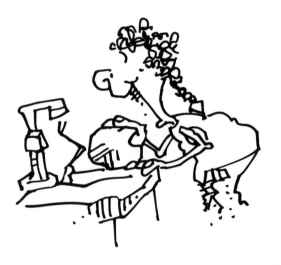

3. Here's where the dancing part comes in. Turn on the CD player and have some cool music cued up. As the music starts to play, move the balloon back and forth toward the stream of water with the beat of the music. The stream of water will respond to the electrostatic charge on the balloon and wiggle back and forth to the beat and look like they are dancing along with the music. Ham it up.

Things I've Screwed Up

We have the papa bear and mama bear syndrome going here again. The stream of water must be continuous for this to be an effective demonstration. Too little and it won't work, and if it is too much, you won't see very much movement either. It has got to be just right.

Also, if you get your balloon wet, you are going to have to dry it off and start all over. Not a huge problem, but it does put a dent in the continuity of the presentation.

How Come, Huh?

The negative charge on the balloon repelled the negatively charged oxygen atoms and attracted the positively charged hydrogen atoms. Since water is a liquid, it is free to bend, move, and respond to the electric charge.

The atoms rotate, the positively charged hydrogen atoms are attracted to the negatively charged balloon and move toward it.

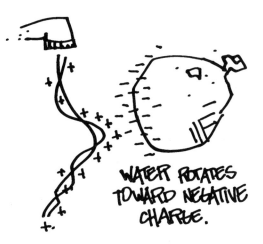

WATER ROTATES TOWARD NEGATIVE CHARGE.

Take It & Run with It

64. Fill a pie tin full of water and see if bringing a negatively charged balloon near the surface affects the water in any way. See if it is possible to create waves by moving the balloon up and down over the surface of the water.

65. Substitute a powerful magnet for the charged balloon and see if the magnet will attract the water molecules in the same way that the balloon did.

Ping-Pong Directives

A Little Background

OK, water is easy. You did that. How about something much heavier? In this lab you are going to use static electricity to attract and move a Ping-Pong ball around a hard, smooth table at your command. Magic? Nope, just science.

Setting the Trap ...

Much like your trained water faucet and obedient bubbles you can announce that you have trained Ping-Pong balls that come to you on command.

Props

1   Ping-Pong ball
1   Hard, smooth surface
1   Balloon, 9 inches, round
1   Pile of hair, fine

The Zing!

1. Find a nice, hard, smooth, level surface and place a Ping-Pong ball in the middle. If it does not start to roll around, you have selected the perfect place.

2.   Inflate a rubber balloon and tie it off. Rub it back and forth vigorously on the head of a person with fine hair. You should be a pro at this by now.

3.   Bring the balloon near the Ping-Pong ball, but do not touch it. The ball should be attracted to the balloon and start to roll in that direction. Once you get the ball rolling, no pun intended, you can direct it anywhere on the table that you want.

BALLOON

BALL

How Come, Huh?

By now, the huge electric charge on the balloon should be extremely familiar to you. This experiment is very similar to the labs where you were wiggling water and getting hair to stand on end. The negative charge on the balloon shoves the negative charges in the Ping-Pong ball atoms away. This exposes the postively charged centers of the Ping-Pong ball atoms—which are attracted to the huge negative charge on the balloon. So, the ball begins to roll …

This is where inertia and mechanics take over a bit. Once the ball starts rolling, it has momentum. The attraction to the negative charge simply causes the ball to have more energy and roll faster. As long as the balloon is tugging at the ball, it will continue to move along a hard, flat surface.

If you remove the balloon, the ball will continue to roll in a straight line until friction and gravity rob all of the momentum from the ball and it eventually stops—until the next charged balloon happens by.

Take It & Run with It

66. Try jumping paper chunks and styrofoam packing peanuts. We are sure that this is not an exhaustive list. Use your imagination and find other things that are attracted to electric charges and will move, jump, or stick.

Splitting Water

A Little Background

Atoms are held together by connections called bonds. When other chemicals come along, these bonds can be broken in favor of making new bonds. This is how new compounds are formed.

Molecules, groups of atoms, can also be split apart using electricity. In this lab you are going to use water to conduct electricity from one pole to another. In the process, water will be split into the two atoms that make it up, hydrogen and oxygen.

Setting the Trap ...

Hold up a glass of water and tell your friends that you are going to decompose the water (split it into pieces) by running electricity through it. Take a drink if the beaker is clean. Not only are you going to split the water in half, but you are also going to put two tubes in the same beaker of water and collect two tubes of gas. But despite the fact that gas is made from the same beaker of water, each tube has a very different reaction to fire. One gas will cause a smoldering stick to burst into flames, and the other tube will cause a burning stick to be extinguished immediately with a pop. Both out of the same beaker of water.

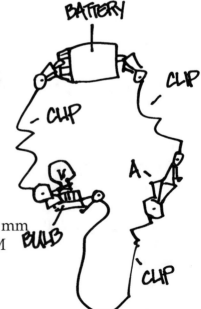

Props

1   500-ml Beaker
1   6-volt Battery
2   Alligator clips
2   Test tubes, 20 mm by 150 mm
1   Bottle of sulfuric acid, 18M
1   Book of matches
2   Wood splints
    Water
    Adult Supervision

The Zing!

1. Add 350 ml of water to the beaker.

2. Connect one alligator clip to each terminal on the top of the battery. Put the loose ends in the beaker.

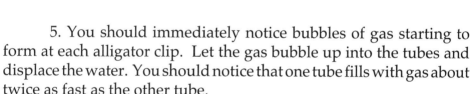

3. Fill the test tubes full of water and invert them in the beaker of water. Insert one alligator clip into the opening of each tube.

4. Add a dash of sulfuric acid to the water and swirl it around a bit to mix it in with the water.

5. You should immediately notice bubbles of gas starting to form at each alligator clip. Let the gas bubble up into the tubes and displace the water. You should notice that one tube fills with gas about twice as fast as the other tube.

6. When the tubes are at least three-fourths full of gas, light one of the splints on fire. Grab the test tube that has the least amount of gas in the beaker. Quickly blow the splint out, lift the tube up, and immediately insert the burning splint in the test tube. If everything is going according to Hoyle, the splint will burst into flames.

7. Take the burning splint and quickly remove the other test tube. Insert the splint inside the second tube, and you will notice that there is a loud pop and the flame on the splint is extinguished. Two tubes, same beaker of water, two different reactions. This definitely poses some food for thought.

Splitting Water

How Come, I've Screwed Things Up, Huh?

There are several things that can go wrong with this experiment, as we know all too well. To explain what to do and why stuff is doing what stuff is doing we have combined two sections into one for this experiment only.

1. If the alligator clips are shoved too far up into the tubes, the movement of electrons through the water, and as a result, the actual splitting of the water molecule into gases is diminished. Make sure the alligator clips have a clear pathway to one another.

2. The tube with the least amount of gas is pure oxygen. It causes the burning splint to burst into flames. When you lift the tube up out of the water, you want to make it a smooth, simple motion. The second that you have the end of the tube out of the water turn the tube sideways and insert the burning splint. If you fiddle and fool at all, the gas will flow out of the tube, and you will lose the ability to create the reaction.

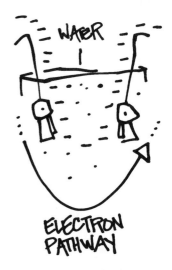

3. With the other tube you have pure hydrogen—a gas lighter than air. Lift the tube straight up and leave it upside down, trapping the lighter hydrogen gas up in the tube. Hydrogen gas is also flammable. When you are ready to insert the burning splint, quickly turn the tube right side up and hold the splint in the top of the tube. The hydrogen gas, being lighter than air will float up and come in contact with the flame. When it does, it will spontaneously ignite and burn the remainder of the gas down inside the tube. This heats the air inside the tube, causing it to expand rapidly, rushing out of the tube, making a whoop and extinguishing the flame all in about two-thirds of a second.

Van de 'Do

A Little Background

You are going to create the world's wildest hairdo courtesy of several billion electrons on the loose. An assistant, one, who preferably, has fine, shoulder-length hair is going to place her hand on the top of the Van de Graaff machine. When you flip the switch, the electrons will start to flow, and upon completely saturating your assistant's body, will produce a hairdo that stands out among its peers—pun intended.

Setting the Trap ...

Invite a friend to be in your demonstration. Have her stand on a a milk crate and ask her if she believes in ghosts. Regardless of the answer, inform her that you are going to conduct a paranormal scientific experiment and check her to see if she believes in apparitions, poltergeists, ghosts, ghouls, and other assorted residents of Hollywood and lower Transylvania.

Props

1 Van de Graaff generator
1 Discharge wand
1 Milk crate, plastic
1 Volunteer, fine hair

Van de 'Do

The Zing!

1. Check to make sure that the machine is off.

2. Ask your assistant to climb up on the milk crate. Make sure that your assistant is not near any electrical conductors like metal legs on chairs or tables. Ask her if she believes in ghosts.

3. Ask her to place one hand, palm down, on the top of the Van de Graaff. Inform her that the machine can tell the truth about beliefs. If she does believe, then the machine will create a hairdo similar to one that a person has when seeing a ghost, that is if one has actually had this experience. One only knows.
    If she does not believe in ghosts, her hair will remain the same.

4. Flip the switch to the Van de Graaff and turn the knob to increase the speed to about 75-80 percent of the maximum.

5. When you have achieved the desired hairdo, have your assistant keep her hand on the top of the generator and turn the machine off. Observe what happens to the hairdo.

6. Ask your assistant to step down off the milk crate anytime after you turn the machine off.

7. Repeat the experiment with friends who have different colors of hair, different thicknesses of hair, and different types of hair— curly, kinky, straight, and wavy.

Things I've Screwed Up

Do this on a day where the humidity is low.

How Come, Huh?

What you should have found was that kids with fine, straight hair had the largest reaction to the Van de Graaff generator.

The Van de Graaff generates billions of electrons that are in a very mobile state. The human body is an excellent conduit for moving electricity around, so the electrons that find their way to the surface of the Van de Graaff race onto the assistant's arm and over to her body.

Once the electrons are on her body, they race all over and saturate everything including the hair shafts. Because electrons have a negative charge, the hair is full of negatively charged electrons, and we know that like charges repel, the hair shafts stand on end trying to get away from one another.

When your volunteer takes her hand off the Van de Graaff, the source of electrons saturating her body dries up and the electrons on your assistant's body start to jump ship. As more and more electrons leave, the charge in the hair is reduced and everything starts to head toward normal. When your assistant jumps onto the ground, the remaining electrons are conducted down to the Earth, which flattens the hair.

Take It & Run with It

67. Hey, how about those guys who get hair transplants, plugs, weaves, and other assorted attachments. Herd a bunch of old, formerly bald guys into the lab and see how they do with extra electrons.

Hole in One

A Little Background

Snap the small plastic dowel off the inside of the ring. Balance the ring on the mouth of the pop bottle and place the plastic dowel directly on top of the ring. The whole set up should look something like the illustration to the right.

Your task, the proverbial challenge as it may be, is to remove the ring from the top of the bottle in such a manner that the plastic dowel falls directly and succinctly into the pop bottle. Call it a hole in one, a shot down the middle, or threading the proverbial physics needle, we don't care—just get the dowel in the bottle. One clue, use the principle of Newton's first law.

Setting the Trap ...

Larry Bird won a lot money from beat reporters covering the NBA in his day. During warm-ups before the game he would shoot several three-point shots and deliberately miss more than he made. He would turn to the rookie reporters sitting on the sideline watching Bird warm up and bet them fifty bucks that he would make the next shot... from ten feet behind the three-point line. Occasionally, a reporter would bite, seeing Bird miss several, and ante up the fifty. With the fish on the hook, Bird would take the ball and drill the three pointer and collect the money. We will use the same bait and switch approach to teach physics.

Props

1 1/2 inch Piece of plastic dowel
1 Soda pop bottle, empty, clean
1 5-inch Diameter plastic ring, 0.5 inch thick

The Zing!

1. With your friends watching set the plastic ring on the bottle opening. Balance the dowel on the very top of the ring directly over the opening of the hole. Use the illustration to the right as a guide.

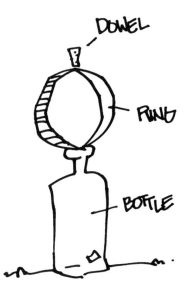

2. This is where you do your best Larry Bird impression. Tell your friends that today, in honor of Sir Isaac Newton and his first law, you are going to play a game that demonstrates inertia. The object of the game is to remove the ring and have the dowel fall directly into the bottle. Demonstrate in slow motion.

3. Replace the ring and dowel. Theatrically, whap the outside of the ring several times, causing the dowel to pop up in the air. Your obvious lack of success should be very noticeable to your buddies. After three or four unsuccessful attempts stop and up the ante. Bet them something that they can offer as a group and probably don't want to lose. For example, if the dowel goes in, they clean your room after school; if you miss, you make popcorn for everyone and they get to spend the day watching a video or DVD of their choice at your expense. Something like that.

Hole in One

4. It is money time. When you go to knock the ring out of the way this time, you will want to pass by the outside edge and whap the ring in the middle. This flattens the ring while you move it out of the way and allows the dowel to fall directly into the opening of the bottle. Everyone groans, you get a clean room and Larry Bird is somewhere in Indiana smiling.

Things I've Screwed Up

I have demonstrated this lab idea for years and still don't always get the dowel to fall into the bottle. Practice. Sometimes it helps to fatigue the plastic a bit by repeatedly squishing to make it softer and more pliable.

If you are having real trouble, try a half-gallon, glass, orange juice bottle or one of these new tea bottles with the wide mouth. As long as you hit the inside of the ring, you will be successful; and as long as they hit the outside of the ring, the dowel will pop into the air.

How Come, Huh?

When the ring is hit on the outside edge, the force from your finger causes the ring to compress upward. The upward movement of the plastic is transferred to the dowel, which shoots up into the air. It is possible that the dowel would then fall directly into the pop bottle, but in 15 years of doing this demonstration, we are 0 for 24,718.

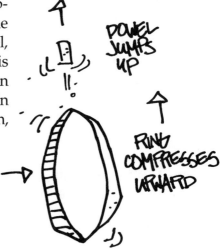

STRIKE OUTSIDE OF RING

DOWEL JUMPS UP

RING COMPRESSES UPWARD

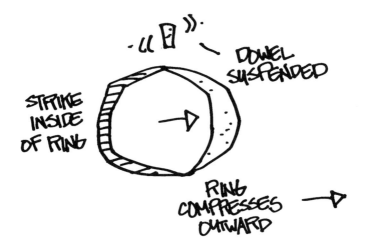

STRIKE INSIDE OF RING

DOWEL SUSPENDED

RING COMPRESSES OUTWARD

The more predictable method of solving this puzzle is to pass by the outside of the ring and whack the inside of the ring. This stretches the ring outward, which produces an interesting result from the dowel's point of view. It is experiencing Newton's first law.

One minute the dowel is resting comfortably on its perch above the bottle. The next minute it is suspended in midair with absolutely nothing underneath it. The ring is removed without disturbing the dowel, much like pulling a tablecloth out from under a pile of dishes. It happens so quickly that none of the energy is transferred from the tablecloth to the dishes or, in this case, the ring to the dowel.

GRAVITY PULLS DOWEL DOWN

The end result is that the ring is gone, the dowel is in midair thanks to its inertia, and the bottle is directly below, perfectly lined up for a hole in one. Gravity takes over, tugs the dowel straight down, and with no other forces to disrupt its path, it falls directly into the bottle—most of the time.

Take It & Run with It

68. Supersize this experiment. Use a 5-gallon water bottle, giant ring made from a plastic barrel or drum, and a huge wooden dowel. Same concept, same outcome, just easier to see.

Balancing Stick

A Little Background

You will find a large, plastic stick that looks like a craft stick with a groove cut in it. Your task is to get this thing that we call a balancing stick to balance vertically on your fingertip. Like the cartoon to the right. It will take finding and altering the center of gravity to do the trick.

Setting the Trap ...

Pass the sticks out and tell your friends that whoever can balance the stick on the end of their finger longer than 4 seconds gets a candy bar; longer than 6 seconds and they get a soda; and if they can make it all the way to 8 seconds, they get a bag of popcorn and a free pass to the next Bull Riders only event.

Oh, and did we mention that anyone who could balance their stick longer than you gets an automatic noogie. Pass the sticks out and let the competition begin.

Props

1   Plastic balancing stick or popsicle stick
1   16-inch Piece of bell wire
6   Large washers
1   Finger

The Zing!

1. When you place the balancing stick on the end of your finger, it will almost immediately start to fall and be very difficult to balance. The reason for this is that the center of gravity is directly above your finger in the center of the stick and that center of gravity wants to fall toward your finger.

2. Bend the bell wire in half and wrap it around the notches that are found near the bottom of the stick. The groove in the plastic balancing stick is designed so that you can wrap a loop of copper wire around it.

3. Bend the ends of the wire into a "U" shape and hang 3 washers off each end of the wire.

4. With the added weight, balance the end of the stick on your finger. You should have better luck—the lower the center of gravity, the easier it is to balance an object. Lower the center of gravity below the focal point and you are actually creating a downward force to counteract the pull of gravity.

Circus performers who walk on the high wire carry a large, flexible pole. The ends of the pole actually droop below the level of the wire. This lowers the center of gravity for the wire walker and actually makes it much easier for him or her to balance.

5. Needless to say, if your friends are trying to balance the stick with no assistance, and you are walking around the room with the stick not only balanced but staying in place as you walk, you will be accused of cheating, playing unfair, and generally behaving in an improper manner for an underage juvenile. All true.

Balancing Stick

Things I've Screwed Up

If you do not have enough weight hanging from the wires, this experiment will not work.

How Come, Huh?

Trying to balance the stick before you added the washers is almost impossible. The entire weight of the stick is above your finger and that weight, pulled by gravity, tends to make the stick fall over.

By wrapping the wire and placing the washers where you did, two things happened. One, you lowered the center of gravity to a point under your finger; and two, this means that there is weight pulling down on the stick when there wasn't any before. This weight created a pair of downward forces that were strong enough to prevent the stick from falling over. The more weight that you add, the more stable the stick becomes. Don't believe me? Try it.

Take It & Run with It

69. Experiment with the amount of weight you hang off the wire and the stability of the stick.

70. Try getting the stick to hang horizontally from your fingertip.

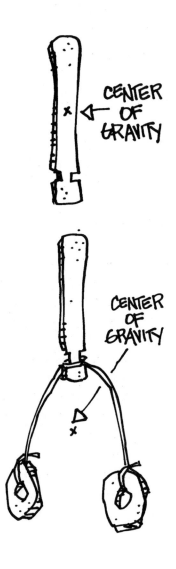

Energy Discs

A Little Background

There is a great physics toy that is manufactured in great quantity in China and imported to the USA by boatloads. It consists of a plastic sphere that is cut in half. When the sphere is inverted and placed on a hard surface, the potential energy that was stored inside the disc is released as kinetic energy—when the disc pops into the air. Great way to learn about stored energy, energy transfer, and spontaneous laughter during lab.

Setting the Trap ...

Give each kid at your science party an energy disc. This is the challenge, tell them that they must place it on the table so it hops into the air about 3 feet. A couple of caveats and exceptions:

a. You may not place the disc on anything other than a hard surface: no mousetraps, explosives, sleeping crickets, or anything else that would cause the plastic to jump into the air.

b. You may not drop the disc on to a hard surface in combination with anything else. It must simply start on the table and hop into the air of its own accord.

c. You may not strike the table or hard surface from underneath.

Props

1 Popper
1 Hard surface

Energy Discs

The Zing!

Flip the energy disc inside out and place it on the table. The plastic has memory. When it snaps back into shape, it will shoot into the air.

Things I've Screwed Up

1. When these are fresh out of the bag, they snap back to their original shape very quickly—so quickly, sometimes, that you cannot even place them on the table. To alleviate this problem, fold the energy disc in half and then twist it 15 to 20 times. This fatigues the plastic and makes it easier for you to set the disc on the table.

2. Occasionally your pal will have a terrible time getting the disc to pop into the air. All it does is snap and move a small distance. Flip the disc over and put the other surface on the table. He had it upside down.

STORED POTENTIAL ENERGY

INSIDE OUT POPPER

How Come, Huh?

The plastic disc has a "memory" or a shape that it is most comfortable in. When you flipped the disc inside out, it took energy from your muscles for you to do this. When you added this energy to the disc, it was stored in the plastic as potential energy or p.e. This is energy that is sitting there waiting to be used, but in the meantime, it will be happy to just hang out.

If you watched the inverted disc carefully, you could see it slowly moving back toward its original, preferred shape. It was using the potential energy you gave it to return to its original shape. As it got closer and closer to the shape, the changes came faster and faster until at the very end, the disc snapped right back into its original shape very quickly.

This final snap created a force against the table—an action. The table, having both read up on Newton's third law of action and reaction and not wanting to be perceived as a wimp, smacked the disc back—a reaction, a bit impetuous perhaps, but a reaction. Newton observed it this way: "For every action there is an equal and opposite reaction." The disc smacks the table, the table smacks the disc back. Basically, nursery school physics. The thing to remember is that the mass of the disc and the amount of energy stored in the disc is very small compared to the mass of the table. When the disc smacks the table, the table simply returns the same amount of energy. This force, fairly significant as far as the disc is concerned, sends it sailing into the air.

Take It & Run with It

71. Try your popper on lots of different surfaces and collect as much data as you can to determine a rule for how poppers behave.

Ping-Pong Poppers

A Little Background

As you learned in the previous zinger, when energy is stored in a material as potential energy, it can then later release that as kinetic energy. The material that the popper is made out of is very flexible and can be shaped and bent into a variety of positions. By bending and shaping the popper, you are actually adding potential energy to the popper.

The plastic has a memory. If it is bent or shaped one way and then left alone, it tends to release the energy that shaped it and return to its original shape. When this happens, the plastic sphere transfers some of the stored potential energy to the Ping-Pong ball that is resting comfortably inside it. The response of the ball, of course, is the direction that we want to head in.

Setting the Trap ...

An extension of the preceding lab and one that should be pretty easy to solve. Find the Ping-Pong ball that is in your collection of materials and place it on the table, so it hops into the air at least three feet. A couple of caveats and exceptions:

a. You may not drop the ball onto a hard surface in combination with anything else. It must simply start on the table and hop into the air of its own accord.

b. You may not strike the table or hard surface from underneath.

Props

1   Popper
1   Hard surface
1   Ping-Pong ball
1   Pair of goggles

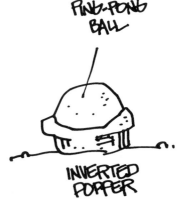

PING-PONG BALL

INVERTED POPPER

The Zing!

1. As with the previous experiment, flip the disc inside out and set it on a hard surface. Only this time, set the disc upside down so that it creates a little bowl.

2. Goggle up and quickly place the Ping-Pong ball inside the bowl and observe what happens when the potential energy is released. Did we mention to duck?

Things I've Screwed Up

1. If you have not read the previous lab, then you would need to know that when these are fresh out of the bag, they snap back to their original shape very quickly—so quickly, some times, that you cannot even place them on the table. To alleviate this problem fold the energy disc in half and then twist it 15 to 20 times. This fatigues the plastic and makes it easier for you to set the disc on the table.

2. The Ping-Pong balls are going to be flying all over the place. Goggles are usually suggested for most science lab activities, but I would say that for this one you really want to consider passing out the eye protection.

3. And, finally, some kids flip the disc upside down, the wrong way with this experiment too. The Ping-Pong ball usually just rolls out of the popper and onto the floor. Have them flip it over.

Ping-Pong Poppers

How Come, Huh?

The plastic disc still has a "memory" or a shape that it is most comfortable in. When you added this energy to the disc, it was stored in the plastic as potential energy. Nothing has changed too much from the previous experiment—except that the disc is upside down but still wants to return to its original shape.

When the disc finally does return to its original shape, it transfers the energy that you stored in it to the ball, instead of the table. A combination of Newton's second law: F=ma and third law, or, "The more force on an object, the more it accelerates. But the more massive it is, the more it resists acceleration," and, "For every action there is an equal and opposite reaction."

The disc smacks the ball: action. The ball shoots into the air, reaction. The fact that the ball is so light figures

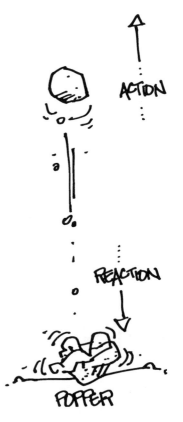

into the F=ma equation. Force equals the mass times the acceleration. Or, if we wiggle the equation around a bit: a=F/m, the acceleration of the ball equals the force of the popper smacking the ball divided by the mass of the ball. In this case, the ball is very light so the bottom number is small and the ball shoots way up into the air—as you probably observed.

The rest of the story is that the ball shoots as high as it can until the pull of gravity overcomes the force that was applied by the popper or it hits the ceiling. When that happens, the ball falls to the Earth and generally rolls under the refrigerator—at least it works that way in our house.

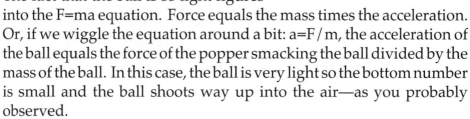

That's it, you've made it to the end of the book, and if you explored along the way, your universe is richer and more diverse than when you started. Join us for another book when you get the chance, we're off to the beach to catch some killer tubes, dude!

Science Fair Projects
•
A Step-by-Step Guide: From Idea To Presentation

Science Fair Projects

Ah, the impending science fair project—a good science fair project has the following five characteristics:

1. The student must come up with an *original* question.

2. That *original* question must be suited to an experiment in order to provide an answer.

3. The *original* idea is outlined with just one variable isolated.

4. The *original* experiment is performed and documented using the scientific method.

5. A presentation of the *original* idea in the form of a lab write-up and display board is completed.

Science Fair Projects

As simple as science fair versus science project sounds, it gets screwed up millions of times a year by sweet, unsuspecting students who are counseled by sweet, unknowing, and probably just as confused parents.

To give you a sense of contrast we have provided a list of legitimate science fair projects and then reports that do not qualify. We will also add some comments in italics that should help clarify why they do or do not qualify in the science fair project department.

Science Fair Projects

1. Temperature and the amount of time it takes mealworms to change to beetles.

Great start. We have chosen a single variable that is easy to measure: temperature. From this point forward the student can read, explore, and formulate an original question that is the foundation for the project.

A colleague of mine actually did a similar type of experiment for his master's degree. His topic: The rate of development of fly larva in cow poop as a function of temperature. No kidding. He found out that the warmer the temperature of the poop the faster the larva developed into flies.

2. The effect of different concentrations of soapy water on seed germination.

Again, wonderful. Measuring the concentration of soapy water. This leads naturally into original questions and a good project.

3. Crystal size and the amount of sugar in the solution.

This could lead into other factors such as exploring the temperature of the solution, the size of the solution container, and other variables that may affect crystal growth. Opens a lot of doors.

50 Science Zingers! • Hixson

vs. Science Reports

4. Helicopter rotor size and the speed at which it falls.

Size also means surface area, which is very easy to measure. The student who did this not only found the mathematical threshold with relationship to air friction, but she had a ton of fun.

5. The ideal ratio of baking soda to vinegar to make a fire extinguisher.

Another great start. Easy to measure and track, leads to a logical question that can either be supported or refuted with the data.

Each of those topics *measures* one thing such as the amount of sugar, the concentration of soapy water, or the ideal size. If you start with an idea that allows you to measure something, then you can change it, ask questions, explore, and ultimately make a *prediction*, also called a *hypothesis*, and experiment to find out if you are correct. Here are some well-meaning but misguided entries:

Science Reports, <u>not Projects</u>
1. Dinosaurs!
OK, great. Everyone loves dinosaurs but where is the experiment? Did you find a new dinosaur? Is Jurassic Park alive and well, and we are headed there to breed, drug, or in some way test them? Probably not. This was a report on T. rex. Cool, but not a science fair project. And judging by the protest that this kid's mom put up when the kid didn't get his usual "A", it is a safe bet that she put a lot of time in and shared in the disappointment.

More Reports &

2. Our Friend the Sun

Another very large topic, no pun intended. This could be a great topic. Sunlight is fascinating. It can be split, polarized, reflected, refracted, measured, collected, converted. However, this poor kid simply chose to write about the size of the sun, regurgitating facts about its features, cycles, and other astrofacts while simultaneously offending the American Melanoma Survivors Society. Just kidding about that last part.

3. Smokers' Poll

A lot of folks think that they are headed in the right direction here. Again, it depends on how the kid attacks the idea. Are they going to single out race? Heredity? Shoe size? What exactly are they after here? The young lady who did this report chose to make it more of a psychology-studies effort than a scientific report. She wanted to know family income, if they fought with their parents, how much stress was on the job, and so on. All legitimate concerns but not placed in the right slot.

4. The Majestic Moose

If you went out and caught the moose, drugged it to see the side effects for disease control, or even mated it with an elk to determine if you could create an animal that would become the spokesanimal for the Alabama Dairy Farmers' Got Melk? promotion, that would be fine. But, another fact-filled report should be filed with the English teacher.

5. How Tadpoles Change into Frogs

Great start, but they forgot to finish the statement. We know how tadpoles change into frogs. What we don't know is how tadpoles change into frogs if they are in an altered environment, if they are hatched out of cycle, if they are stuck under the tire of an off-road vehicle blatantly driving through a protected wetland area. That's what we want to know. How tadpoles change into frogs, if, when, or under what measurable circumstances.

Now that we have beat the chicken squat out of this introduction, we are going to show you how to pick a topic that can be adapted to become a successful science fair project after one more thought.

One Final Comment

A Gentle Reminder

Quite often I discuss the scientific method with moms and dads, teachers and kids, and get the impression that, according to their understanding, there is one, and only one, scientific method. This is not necessarily true. There are lots of ways to investigate the world we live in and on.

Paleontologists dig up dead animals and plants but have no way to conduct experiments on them. They're dead. Albert Einstein, the most famous scientist of the last century and probably on everybody's starting five of all time, never did experiments. He was a theoretical physicist, which means that he came up with a hypothesis, skipped over collecting materials for things like black holes and space-time continuums, didn't experiment on anything or even collect data. He just went straight from hypothesis to conclusion, and he's still considered part of the scientific community. You'll probably follow the six steps we outline but keep an open mind.

Project Planner

This outline is designed to give you a specific set of time lines to follow as you develop your science fair project. Most teachers will give you 8 to 11 weeks notice for this kind of assignment. We are going to operate from the shorter time line with our suggested schedule, which means that the first thing you need to do is get a calendar.

A. The suggested time to be devoted to each item is listed in parentheses next to that item. Enter the date of the Science Fair and then, using the calendar, work backward entering dates.

B. As you complete each item, enter the date that you completed it in the column between the goal (due date) and project item.

Goal   *Completed*   *Project Item*

1. Generate a Hypothesis (2 weeks)

_____ _____	Review Idea Section, pp. 194–200
_____ _____	Try Several Experiments
_____ _____	Hypothesis Generated
_____ _____	Finished Hypothesis Submitted
_____ _____	Hypothesis Approved

2. Gather Background Information (1 week)

_____ _____	Concepts/Discoveries Written Up
_____ _____	Vocabulary/Glossary Completed
_____ _____	Famous Scientists in Field

& Time Line

Goal   *Completed*   *Project Item*

3. Design an Experiment (1 week)

_____   _____   Procedure Written
_____   _____   Lab Safety Review Completed
_____   _____   Procedure Approved
_____   _____   Data Tables Prepared
_____   _____   Materials List Completed
_____   _____   Materials Acquired

4. Perform the Experiment (2 weeks)

_____   _____   Scheduled Lab Time

5. Collect and Record Experimental Data (part of 4)

_____   _____   Data Tables Completed
_____   _____   Graphs Completed
_____   _____   Other Data Collected and Prepared

6. Present Your Findings (2 weeks)

_____   _____   Rough Draft of Paper Completed
_____   _____   Proofreading Completed
_____   _____   Final Report Completed
_____   _____   Display Completed
_____   _____   Oral Report Outlined on Index Cards
_____   _____   Practice Presentation of Oral Report
_____   _____   Oral Report Presentation
_____   _____   Science Fair Setup
_____   _____   Show Time!

Scientific Method
• Step 1 •
The Hypothesis

The Hypothesis

A hypothesis is an educated guess. It is a statement of what you think will probably happen. It is also the most important part of your science fair project because it directs the entire process. It determines what you study, the materials you will need, and how the experiment will be designed, carried out, and evaluated. Needless to say, you need to put some thought into this part.

There are four steps to generating a hypothesis:

Step One • Pick a Topic
Preferably something that you are interested in studying. We would like to politely recommend that you take a peek at physical science ideas (physics and chemistry) if you are a rookie and this is one of your first shots at a science fair project. These kinds of lab ideas allow you to repeat experiments quickly. There is a lot of data that can be collected, and there is a huge variety to choose from.

If you are having trouble finding an idea, all you have to do is pick up a compilation of science activities (like this one) and start thumbing through it. Go to the local library or head to a bookstore and you will find a wide and ever-changing selection to choose from. Find a topic that interests you and start reading. At some point an idea will catch your eye, and you will be off to the races.

Pick a Topic ...

We hope you find an idea you like between the covers of this book. But we also realize that 1) there are more ideas about physical science than we have included in this book and 2) other kinds of presentations, or methods of writing labs, may be just what you need to trigger a new idea or put a different spin on things. So, without further adieu, we introduce you to several additional titles that may be of help to you in developing a science fair project.

1. You Gotta Try This, Absolutely Irresistible Science. Written by Vicki Cobb and Kathy Darling, illustrated by True Kelley ISBN 0-688-15740-8 Published by Morrow Junior Books. 144 pages.

Vicki Cobb is one of my favorite authors. She presents her lab ideas in a clear and concise manner and has understandable and scientifically sound explanations. This particular book has a variety of 60 different science experiments listed in categories like: Getting Personal (human biology), Curious Chemistry, Freaky Fluids, and Nuke Knacks (experiments you can do in your microwave). The activities are fun and the illustrations are entertaining.

2. See For Yourself: More than 100 Experiments for Science Fairs and Projects. Written by Vicki Cobb and illustrated by Dave Klug. ISBN 0-439-09010-5. Published by Scholastic. 192 pages.

Another Vicki Cobb book and another collection of 100 fun science experiments. This book is geared more toward guiding the student to completing a science fair project. The book starts with activities about the human body, moves into products that you can find at the supermarket, draws inspiration from the toy store, drugstore, hardware store, and finally, the stationery store. All of these labs introduce you to products that are commonly found in these locations and can be used to demonstrate principles of science. There are sidebars with fun facts, great illustrations, and lots of activities with common, easy-to-find items.

Find an Idea You Like

3. *333 More Science Tricks and Experiments.* Written by Robert J. Brown. ISBN 0-8306-0835-4 Published by TAB Books.   230 pages.

A veritable potpourri of lab activities. Lots and lots of physics activities from the topics of inertia, momentum, sound, water and fluid dynamics, gravity, centrifugal force, and electricity. The book is peppered with illustrations and photographs, the lab activities are written in a no-nonsense, let's-get-to-work kind of way. Some activities are explained in a short paragraph or less. Lots of ideas.

4. *Science in Seconds with Toys: Over 100 Experiments that You Can Do in 10 Minutes or Less.* Written by Jean Potter. ISBN 0-471-17900-0. Published by John Wiley & Sons.   122 pages.

A very kid-friendly book. Each experiment is laid out so that it is easy to read. There are friendly cartoons to help explain what to do and what is going on during the lab.   The book is divided up by sections as to what the toy does: floating, bouncing, plucking, banging, blowing, etc. There is a question, a list of materials, easy-to-follow instructions, and an explanation.

5. *What? For the Young Scientist.* Written by Robert W. Wood. Illustrated by Steve Hoeft. ISBN 0-7910-4847-0. Published by Chelsea House.   144 pages.

Thirty-two experiments written by another very good, and well-known science educator.   Each activity answers a question beginning with "What". For example some of the questions are, "What are lungs for?" and "What are clouds?" Each lab activity starts with a question and is then followed by a list of materials that you can check off as you acquire them, a procedure that tells you what to do, and the results of the experiment are explained. There is a section for further studies, and finally, a did-you-know section full of fun facts.

Develop an Original Idea

Step Two • Do the Lab

Choose a lab activity that looks interesting and try the experiment. Some kids make the mistake of thinking that all you have to do is find a lab in a book, repeat the lab, and you are on the gravy train with biscuit wheels. Your goal is to ask an ORIGINAL question, not repeat an experiment that has been done a bazillion times before.

As you do the lab, be thinking not only about the data you are collecting, but of ways you could adapt or change the experiment to find out new information. The point of the science fair project is to have you become an actual scientist and contribute a little bit of new knowledge to the world.

You know that they don't pay all of those engineers good money to sit around and repeat other people's lab work. The company wants new ideas so if you are able to generate and explore new ideas you become very valuable, not only to that company but to society. It is the question-askers that find cures for diseases, create new materials, figure out ways to make existing machines energy efficient, and change the way that we live. For the purpose of illustration, we are going to take a lab titled, "Prisms, Water Prisms." from another book, *Photon U*, and run it through the rest of the process. The lab uses a tub of water, an ordinary mirror, and light to create a prism that splits the light into the spectrum of a rainbow. Cool. Easy to do. Not expensive and open to all kinds of adaptations, including the four that we discuss on the next page.

Step Three • *Bend, Fold, Spindle, & Mutilate Your Lab*
Once you have picked out an experiment, ask if it is possible to do any of the following things to modify it into an original experiment. You want to try and change the experiment to make it more interesting and find out one new, small piece of information.

Heat it	Freeze it	Reverse it	Double it
Bend it	Invert it	Poison it	Dehydrate it
Drown it	Stretch it	Fold it	Ignite it
Split it	Irradiate it	Oxidize it	Reduce it
Chill it	Speed it up	Color it	Grease it
Expand it	Substitute it	Remove it	Slow it down

If you take a look at our examples, that's exactly what we did to the main idea. We took the list of 24 different things that you could do to an experiment—not nearly all of them by the way—and tried a couple of them out on the prism setup.

Double it: Get a second prism and see if you can continue to separate the colors farther by lining up a second prism in the rainbow of the first.

Reduce it: Figure out a way to gather up the colors that have been produced and mix them back together to produce white light again.

Reverse it: Experiment with moving the flashlight and paper closer to the mirror and farther away. Draw a picture and be able to predict what happens to the size and clarity of the rainbow image.

Substitute it: You can also create a rainbow on a sunny day using a garden hose with a fine-spray nozzle attached. Set the nozzle adjustment so that a fine mist is produced and move the mist around in the sunshine until you see the rainbow. This works better if the sun is lower in the sky; late afternoon is best.

ypothesis Work Sheet

Step Three (Expanded) • *Bend, Fold, Spindle Work Sheet*

This work sheet will give you an opportunity to work through process of creating an original idea.

A. Write down the lab idea that you want to mangle.

_____

_____

_____

_____

B. List the possible variables you could change in the lab.

   i. _____

   ii. _____

   iii. _____

   iv. _____

   v. _____

C'MON. HE SAID TO STRETCH IT.

C. Take one variable listed in section B and apply one of the 24 changes listed below to it. Write that change down and state your new lab idea in the space below. Do that with three more changes.

Heat it	Freeze it	Reverse it	Double it
Bend it	Invert it	Poison it	Dehydrate it
Drown it	Stretch it	Fold it	Ignite it
Split it	Irradiate it	Oxidize it	Reduce it
Chill it	Speed it up	Color it	Grease it
Expand it	Substitute it	Remove it	Slow it down

   i. _____

_____

_____

_____

ii. _____

_____

_____

_____

iii. _____

_____

_____

_____

iv. _____

_____

_____

_____

Step Four • Create an Original Idea— Your Hypothesis

Your hypothesis should be stated as an opinion. You've done the basic experiment, you've made observations, you're not stupid. Put two and two together and make a PREDICTION. Be sure that you are experimenting with just a single variable.

A. State your hypothesis in the space below. List the variable.

i. _____

_____

_____

_____

ii. Variable tested: _____

Sample Hypothesis Work Sheet

On the previous two pages is a work sheet that will help you develop your thoughts and a hypothesis. Here is sample of the finished product to help you understand how to use it.

A. Write down the lab idea that you want to mutilate.
A mirror is placed in a tub of water. A beam of light is focused through the water onto the mirror, producing a rainbow on the wall.

B. List the possible variables you could change in the lab.
   i. **Source of light**
   ii. **The liquid in the tub**
   iii. **The distance from flashlight to mirror**

C. Take one variable listed in section B and apply one of the 24 changes to it. Write that change down and state your new lab idea in the space below.

The shape of the beam of light can be controlled by making and placing cardboard filters over the end of the flashlight. Various shapes such as circles, squares, and slits will produce different quality rainbows.

D. State your hypothesis in the space below. List the variable. Be sure that when you write the hypothesis you are stating an idea and <u>not asking a question.</u>

Hypothesis: The narrower the beam of light the tighter, brighter, and more focused the reflected rainbow will appear.

Variable tested: **The opening on the filter**

Scientific Method
· Step 2 ·
Gather Information

Gather Information

Read about your topic and find out what we already know. Check books, videos, the Internet, and movies, talk with experts in the field, and molest an encyclopedia or two. Gather as much information as you can before you begin planning your experiment.

In particular, there are several things that you will want to pay special attention to and that should accompany any good science fair project.

A. Major Scientific Concepts

Be sure that you research and explain the main idea(s) that is / are driving your experiment. It may be a law of physics or chemical rule or an explanation of an aspect of plant physiology.

B. Scientific Words

As you use scientific terms in your paper, you should also define them in the margins of the paper or in a glossary at the end of the report. You cannot assume that everyone knows about geothermal energy transmutation in sulfur-loving bacterium. Be prepared to define some new terms for them... and scrub your hands really well when you are done if that is your project.

C. Historical Perspective

When did we first learn about this idea, and who is responsible for getting us this far? You need to give a historical perspective with names, dates, countries, awards, and other recognition.

Building a Research Foundation

1. This sheet is designed to help you organize your thoughts and give you some ideas on where to look for information on your topic. When you prepare your lab report, you will want to include the background information outlined below.

    A. *Major Scientific Concepts (Two is plenty.)*

        i. _____

_____

_____

_____

        ii. _____

_____

_____

_____

    B. *Scientific Words (No more than 10)*

        i. _____

        ii. _____

        iii. _____

        iv. _____

        v. _____

        vi. _____

        vii. _____

        viii. _____

        ix. _____

        x. _____

    C. *Historical Perspective*

        Add this as you find it.

2. There are several sources of information that are available to help you fill in the details from the previous page.

   A. *Contemporary Print Resources*
      (Magazines, Newspapers, Journals)
         i. _____
         ii. _____
         iii. _____
         iv. _____
         v. _____
         vi. _____

   B. *Other Print Resources*
      (Books, Encyclopedias, Dictionaries, Textbooks)
         i. _____
         ii. _____
         iii. _____
         iv. _____
         v. _____
         vi. _____

   C. *Celluloid Resources*
      (Films, Filmstrips, Videos)
         i. _____
         ii. _____
         iii. _____
         iv. _____
         v. _____
         vi. _____

D. Electronic Resources:
  (Internet Website Addresses, DVDs, MP3s)

   i. _____

   ii. _____

   iii. _____

   iv. _____

   v. _____

   vi. _____

   vii. _____

   viii. _____

   ix. _____

   x. _____

E. Human Resources
  (Scientists, Engineers, Professionals, Professors, Teachers)

   i. _____

   ii. _____

   iii. _____

   iv. _____

   v. _____

   vi. _____

You may want to keep a record of all of your research and add it to the back of the report as an Appendix. Some teachers who are into volume think this is really cool. Others, like myself, find it a pain in the tuchus. No matter what you do, be sure to keep an accurate record of where you find data. If you quote from a report word for word, be sure to give proper credit with either a footnote or parenthetical reference. This is very important for credibility and accuracy. This is will keep you out of trouble with plagiarism (copying without giving credit).

Scientific Method
• Step 3 •
Design Your Experiment

50 Science Zingers! • Hixson

Acquire Your Lab Materials

The purpose of this section is to help you plan your experiment. You'll make a map of where you are going, how you want to get there, and what you will take along.

List the materials you will need to complete your experiment in the table below. Be sure to list multiples if you will need more than one item. Many science materials double as household items in their spare time. Check around the house before you buy anything from a science supply company or hardware store. For your convenience, we have listed some suppliers on page 19 of this book.

Material	Qty.	Source	$
1.			
2.			
3.			
4.			
5.			
6.			
7.			
8.			
9.			
10.			
11.			
12.			

Total $_____

Outline Your Experiment

This sheet is designed to help you outline your experiment. If you need more space, make a copy of this page to finish your outline. When you are done with this sheet, review it with an adult, make any necessary changes, review safety concerns on the next page, prepare your data tables, gather your equipment, and start to experiment.

In the space below, list what you are going to do in the order you are going to do it.

i. _____

_____

_____

_____

ii. _____

_____

_____

_____

iii. _____

_____

_____

_____

iv. _____

_____

_____

_____

v. _____

_____

_____

_____

Evaluate Safety Concerns

We have included an overall safety section in the front of this book on pages 16–18, but there are some very specific questions you need to ask, and prepare for, depending on the needs of your experiment. If you find that you need to prepare for any of these safety concerns, place a check mark next to the letter.

_____ A. *Goggles & Eyewash Station*
If you are mixing chemicals or working with materials that might splinter or produce flying objects, goggles and an eyewash station or sink with running water should be available.

_____ B. *Ventilation*
If you are mixing chemicals that could produce fire, smoke, fumes, or obnoxious odors, you will need to use a vented hood or go outside and perform the experiment in the fresh air.

_____ C. *Fire Blanket or Fire Extinguisher*
If you are working with potentially combustible chemicals or electricity, a fire blanket and extinguisher nearby are a must.

_____ D. *Chemical Disposal*
If your experiment produces a poisonous chemical or there are chemical-filled tissues (as in dissected animals), you may need to make arrangements to dispose of the by-products from your lab.

_____ E. *Electricity*
If you are working with materials and developing an idea that uses electricity, make sure that the wires are in good repair, that the electrical demand does not exceed the capacity of the supply, and that your work area is grounded.

_____ F. *Emergency Phone Numbers*
Look up and record the following phone numbers for the Fire Department: _____ , Poison Control: _____ , and Hospital: _____. Post them in an easy-to-find location.

Prepare Data Tables

Finally, you will want to prepare your data tables and have them ready to go before you start your experiment. Each data table should be easy to understand and easy for you to use.

A good data table has a **title** that describes the information being collected, and it identifies the **variable** and the **unit** being collected on each data line. The variable is *what* you are measuring and the unit is *how* you are measuring it. They are usually written like this:

Variable (unit), or to give you some examples:

Time (seconds)
Distance (meters)
Electricity (volts)

An example of a well-prepared data table looks like the sample below. We've cut the data table into thirds because the book is too small to display the whole line.

Determining the Boiling Point of Compound X_1

Time (min.)	0	1	2	3	4	5	6
Temp. ($^\circ$C)							

Time (min.)	7	8	9	10	11	12	13
Temp. ($^\circ$C)							

Time (min.)	14	15	16	17	18	19	20
Temp. ($^\circ$C)							

Scientific Method
• Step 4 •
Conduct the Experiment

Lab Time

It's time to get going. You've generated a hypothesis, collected the materials, written out the procedure, checked the safety issues, and prepared your data tables. Fire it up. Here's the short list of things to remember as you experiment.

_____ *A. Follow the Procedure, Record Any Changes*

Follow your own directions specifically as you wrote them. If you find the need to change the procedure once you are into the experiment, that's fine; it's part of the process. Make sure to keep detailed records of the changes. When you repeat the experiment a second or third time, follow the new directions exactly.

_____ *B. Observe Safety Rules*

It's easier to complete the lab activity if you are in the lab rather than the emergency room.

_____ *C. Record Data Immediately*

Collect temperatures, distances, voltages, revolutions, and any other variables and immediately record them into your data table. Do not think you will be able to remember them and fill everything in after the lab is completed.

_____ *D. Repeat the Experiment Several Times*

The more data that you collect, the better. It will give you a larger data base and your averages are more meaningful. As you do multiple experiments, be sure to identify each data set by date and time so you can separate them out.

_____ *E. Prepare for Extended Experiments*

Some experiments require days or weeks to complete, particularly those with plants and animals or the growing of crystals. Prepare a safe place for your materials so your experiment can continue undisturbed while you collect the data. Be sure you've allowed enough time for your due date.

Scientific Method
• Step 5 •
Collect and Display Data

Types of Graphs

This section will give you some ideas on how you can display the information you are going to collect as a graph. A graph is simply a picture of the data that you gathered portrayed in a manner that is quick and easy to reference. There are four kinds of graphs described on the next two pages. If you find you need a leg up in the graphing department, we have a book in the series called *Data Tables & Graphing*. It will guide you through the process.

Line and Bar Graphs

These are the most common kinds of graphs. The most consistent variable is plotted on the "x", or horizontal, axis and the more temperamental variable is plotted along the "y", or vertical, axis. Each data point on a line graph is recorded as a dot on the graph and then all of the dots are connected to form a picture of the data. A bar graph starts on the horizontal axis and moves up to the data line.

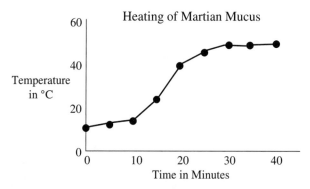

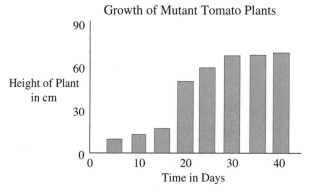

Best Fit Graphs

A best fit graph was created to show averages or trends rather than specific data points. The data that has been collected is plotted on a graph just as on a line graph, but instead of drawing a line from point to point to point, which sometimes is impossible anyway, you just free hand a line that hits "most of the data."

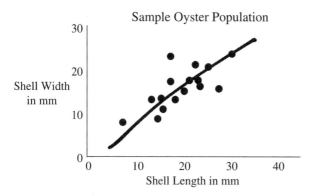

Pie Graphs

Pie graphs are used to show relationships between different groups. All of the data is totaled up and a percentage is determined for each group. The pie is then divided to show the relationship of one group to another.

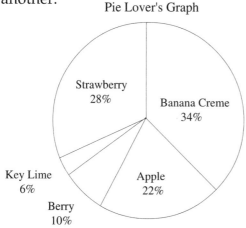

Other Kinds of Data

1. Written Notes & Observations

This is the age-old technique used by all scientists. Record your observations in a lab book. Written notes can be made quickly as the experiment is proceeding, and they can then be expounded upon later. Quite often notes made in the heat of an experiment are revisited during the evaluation portion of the process, and they can shed valuable light on how or why the experiment went the way it did.

2. Drawings

Quick sketches as well as fully developed drawings can be used as a way to report data for a science experiment. Be sure to title each drawing and, if possible, label what it is that you are looking at. Drawings that are actual size are best.

3. Photographs, Videotapes, and Audiotapes

Usually better than drawings, quicker, and more accurate, but you do have the added expense and time of developing the film. However, they can often capture images and details that are not usually seen by the naked eye.

4. The Experiment Itself

Some of the best data you can collect and present is the actual experiment itself. Nothing will speak more effectively for you than the plants you grew, the specimens you collected, or that big pile of tissue that was an armadillo you peeled from the tread of an 18-wheeler.

Scientific Method
• Step 6 •
Present Your Ideas

Oral Report Checklist

It is entirely possible that you will be asked to make an oral presentation to your classmates. This will give you an opportunity to explain what you did and how you did it. Quite often this presentation is part of your overall score, so if you do well, it will enhance your chances for one of the bigger awards.

To prepare for your oral report, your science fair presentation should include the following components:

Physical Display

_____a.   freestanding display board
                      hypothesis
                      data tables, graphs, photos, etc.
                      abstract (short summary)

_____b.   actual lab setup (equipment)

Oral Report

_____a.   hypothesis or question
_____b.   background information
                      concepts
                      word definitions
                      history or scientists
_____c.   experimental procedure
_____d.   data collected
                      data tables
                      graphs
                      photos or drawings
_____e.   conclusions and findings
_____f.   ask for questions

Set the display board up next to you on the table. Transfer the essential information to index cards. Use the index cards for reference, but do not read from them. Speak in a clear voice, hold your head up, and make eye contact with your peers. Ask if there are any questions before you finish and sit down.

Written Report Checklist

Next up is the written report, also called your lab write-up. After you compile or sort the data you have collected during the experiment and evaluate the results, you will be able to come to a conclusion about your hypothesis. Remember, disproving an idea is as valuable as proving it.

This sheet is designed to help you write up your science fair project and present your data in an organized manner. This is a final checklist for you.

To prepare your write-up, your science fair report should include the following components:

_____ a.   binder
_____ b.   cover page, title, & your name
_____ c.   abstract (one paragraph summary)
_____ d.   table of contents with page numbers
_____ e.   hypothesis or question
_____ f.   background information
                      concepts
                      word definitions
                      history or scientists
_____ g.   list of materials used
_____ h.   experimental procedure
                      written description
                      photo or drawing of setup
_____ i.   data collected
                      data tables
                      graphs
                      photos or drawings
_____ j.   conclusions and findings
_____ k.   glossary of terms
_____ l.   references

Display Checklist

2. Prepare your display to accompany the report. A good display should include the following:

Freestanding Display

_____ a.   freestanding cardboard back
_____ b.   title of experiment
_____ c.   your name
_____ d.   hypothesis
_____ e.   findings of the experiment
_____ f.   photo or illustrations of equipment
_____ g.   data tables or graphs

Additional Display Items

_____ h.   a copy of the write-up
_____ i.   actual lab equipment setup

Glossary,
Index,
and
More Ideas

Glossary

Air Pressure

At sea level we have approximately 100 miles of air stacked on top of us. This air is pushing down all the time creating pressure. At sea level it is about 14.7 pounds per square inch. The higher up you go in elevation, the less air is stacked on top of you, the less pressure is squishing you.

Amplification

Increasing the loudness of the sound produced or received. In the case of producing sound, the waves can be focused by a megaphone or other device. In the case of receiving, talk with an elephant.

Bimetallic Strip

A tool composed of two different metal strips attached side by side. When the combined strip is heated in a hot flame, the metals expand at different rates causing the strip to bend. When the curved strip cools, it slowly straightens out and takes its original shape.

Bernoulli's Law

The behavior of fluids as they travel across a surface was first described by an Italian physicist named Bernoulli. He showed that the faster a fluid travels across a surface the less pressure it puts on that surface. That theory is the basis for modern flight.

Charge

The opposite of retreat. But when studying electricity, one tends to think of electrons, which, when they accumulate, have a negative charge. In their absence, a positive charge is created.

Chicken in a Cup

Don't call the PETA folks. This is a string attached to a wax cup. When the string is pulled while it is wet, it produces a squawk that is remarkably similar to a chicken clucking. No real live chickens are harmed or even used for this lab activity.

Conduction

The method that heat uses to move through solid objects. When the heat is absorbed by the solid atoms in one area, they start to vibrate faster and faster, bumping the atoms next to them, bumping the atoms next to them, bumping the atoms next to them, and you get the idea. It is like a pile of dominos falling over. The heat is passed from atom to atom.

Convection Carafe

A large, metal tube with a piece of metal screen stuffed in one end is heated with a propane torch. The screen gets red hot, the tube is removed from the flame, and the tube begins to hum. Grateful that it is no longer being heated? No, a standing wave is set up by the convective air moving through the tube.

Convection Current

This involves the upward movement of warm gases or liquids relative to cooler surrounding gases or liquids. These warmer currents eventually cool and descend. This cyclical movement is called a convection current and is generally the term used to describe how heat moves through liquids and gases.

Density

A measurement that describes how tightly packed a material is. Density is figured out by dividing the mass of the object into the amount of space that it takes up. A common description would be grams per cubic centimeter or pounds per cubic foot. The more tightly packed the substance is, the higher the density.

Dry Ice

Solid carbon dioxide. Don't pop it into your mouth.

Glossary

Doppler Effect

Sound waves produced by a moving object. The faster the object moves toward you, the closer the sound waves are that are produced, giving the illusion of a high-pitched sound. As the object passes, the distance between the waves lengthens, and the sound appears to get lower in pitch.

Electrons

Small, negatively charged particles that are associated with atomic nuclei. They are very small particles and can be swiped very easily from the atoms.

Exothermic Reactions

An exothermic reaction refers to a reaction between two chemicals where heat is produced by the reaction. In this case the two chemicals feel hot to the touch, that is if they have not already burst into flames.

Frequency

A sound wave is measured by the number or beats or pulses it produces per second. The more pulses, the higher the frequency and the higher the pitch of the sound that is produced. In contrast, the slower the frequency of the sound wave, the lower the pitch that is produced.

Index of Refraction

The angle that light is bent when it enters a material that is more or less dense than the material it is traveling in. It is calculated by measuring the change in the speed of light through the material.

Mass

The amount of weight an object has regardless of gravitational attraction or pull.

Matter

Everything that takes up space, regardless of the state that it is in currently, is matter. It can be a solid, liquid, or gas and it can be any temperature.

Motor Effect

The movement of a wire or coil of wires when an electric current is applied to a wire between two magnets. It is the push that gets the coil moving in a real motor.

Nichrome Wire

A metal alloy made of nickel and chromium. This particular metal resists the movement of electrons through it and some of the energy is used to produce heat and light. Your toaster and toaster oven are made using nichrome wires.

Nitinol Wire

Another metal-alloy wire consisting of nichrome—big surprise there—and titanium. The cool thing about this wire is that instead of expanding when it is heated, like most metals, it contracts. This characteristic allows you to bend, mold, twist, and mangle the wire into any shape that you want and it will return to its original shape when heated.

Nucleus

This is the home base of the atom consisting of protons, positively charged particles, and neutrons (particles that have no real opinion on whether they should be charged at all, so they are not). The nucleus of the atom is responsible for 99.9 percent of the mass of the atom and is also how the atomic number is calculated. *Nuclei* is the plural of *nucleus*, a term that originated in Utah in the late 1800s.

Glossary

Pitch

The word that describes how high or how low the sound made by a particular instrument will sound to the ears. If the instrument is short, it produces a high frequency and the pitch will also be high. If the instrument is long, the pitch will be low.

Reflector

A material that bounces or reflects some or all of the light that strikes its surface.

Resonance

Every wave has a particular length. When a container matches the length of the wave, the wave is amplified and sounds much louder than it would in other-sized instruments. When this happens, scientists call it finding the resonant length. If a container matches the sound wave produced in a room, it will also resonate.

Ring & Ball

An instructional tool composed of two instruments. A metal ring on the end of a long, thick wire and a solid, metal ball on the end of a long, thick wire. When both elements are at room temperature, the ball will fit nicely through the ring. When the ball is heated, it expands—as metal does—to the point where it will no longer fit through the ring.

Singing Rods

Solid aluminum rods that are rubbed with rosin. When the rods are held at their nodal points, usually the middle or the one-quarter spot, and the rods are rubbed, they begin to vibrate. In fact, if you match the speed of the rubbing with the frequency of the wave, you can set up a resonant, standing wave, which is very loud and obnoxious.

Static Electricity

An electrical charge that is accumulated and transferred in a random, unpredictable, and measurable way. Generally, rubbing a plastic or vinyl substance with flannel will gather and collect a large pile of electrons. These electrons are called static electricity, because it is electricity, but you can't control it or get it to move from one place to another very easily.

Sublimation

Sublimation happens when a solid changes directly to a gas without passing through the liquid phase, or if a gas becomes a solid without passing through the liquid phase. In either case the liquid portion of the change is not invited to the party.

Van de Graaff Generator

One of the greatest science toys ever invented. A belt spins around a felt roller. As it spins up into a metal dome, the electrons that are collected by the rubber belt are discharged onto the dome and accumulate. When a conductive material, like a finger, comes in contact with the dome, the electrons jump en masse to the finger and a spark of light, a loud snap, and a startled look can all be seen.

Vacuum

An absence of atmosphere. If the gases in a closed container are removed from that container completely and nothing is left, you have a vacuum. If there is some gas remaining inside the container, you have an area of low pressure unless that container is your brain, then we are back to the vacuum definition.

Vibration

The repetitive movement of an object, back and forth, up and down, in a circular motion. When an object vibrates, it can produce a sound frequency that we may be able to hear. The larger the vibrations, the louder the sound; the faster the vibrations, the higher the pitch of the sound. This is really at the heart of what sound is.

Index

Index

Notes

Notes

Notes

Notes

Notes

Notes

Notes